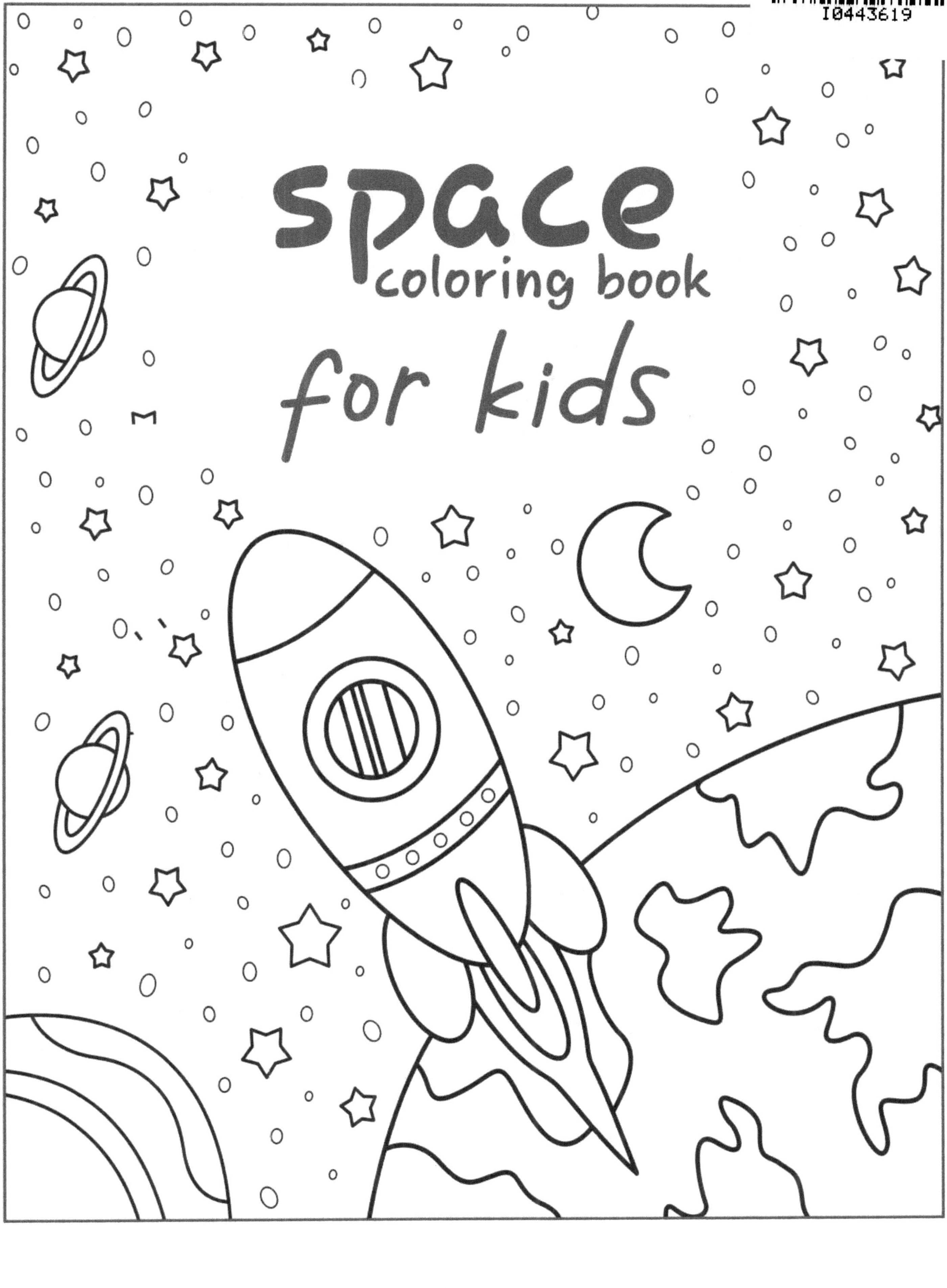
space
coloring book
for kids

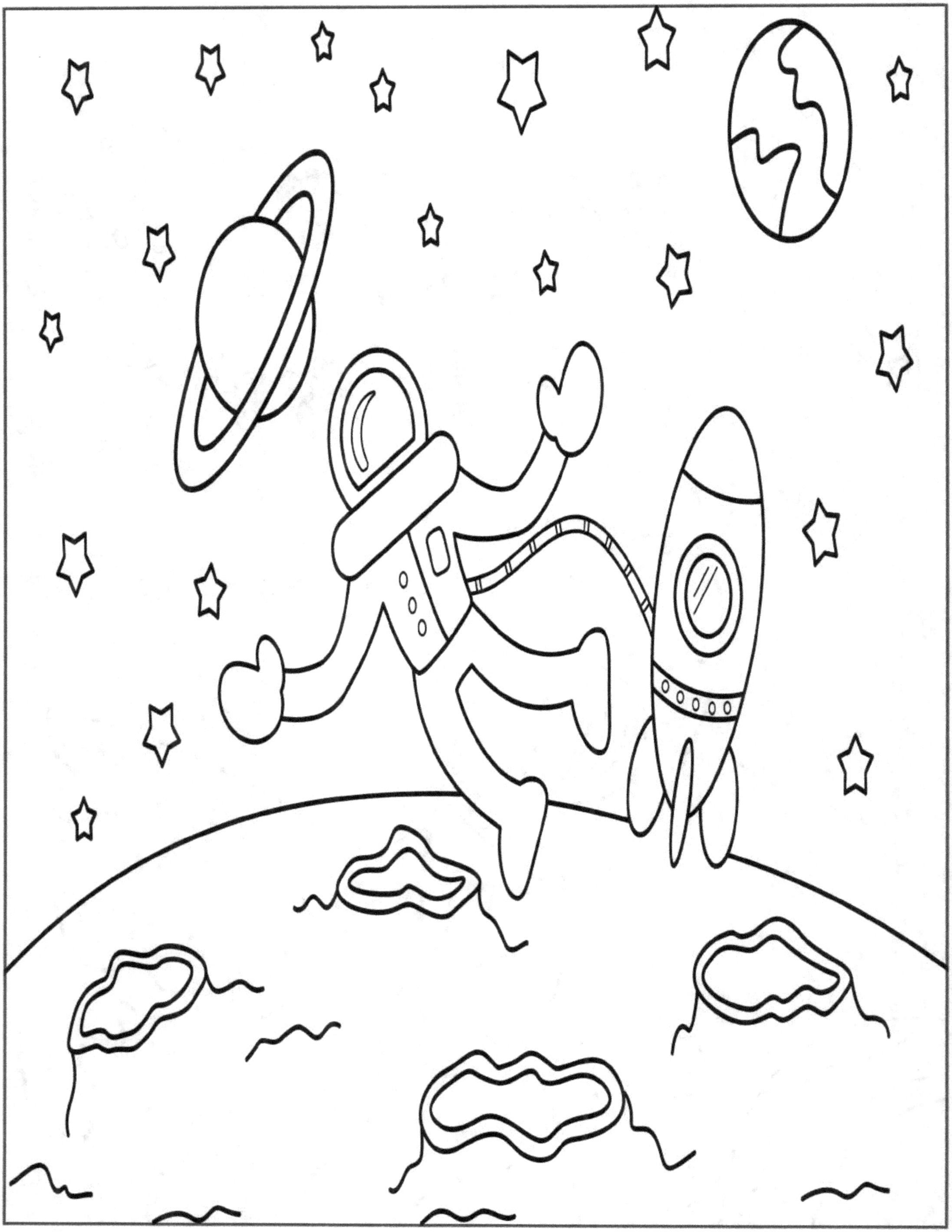

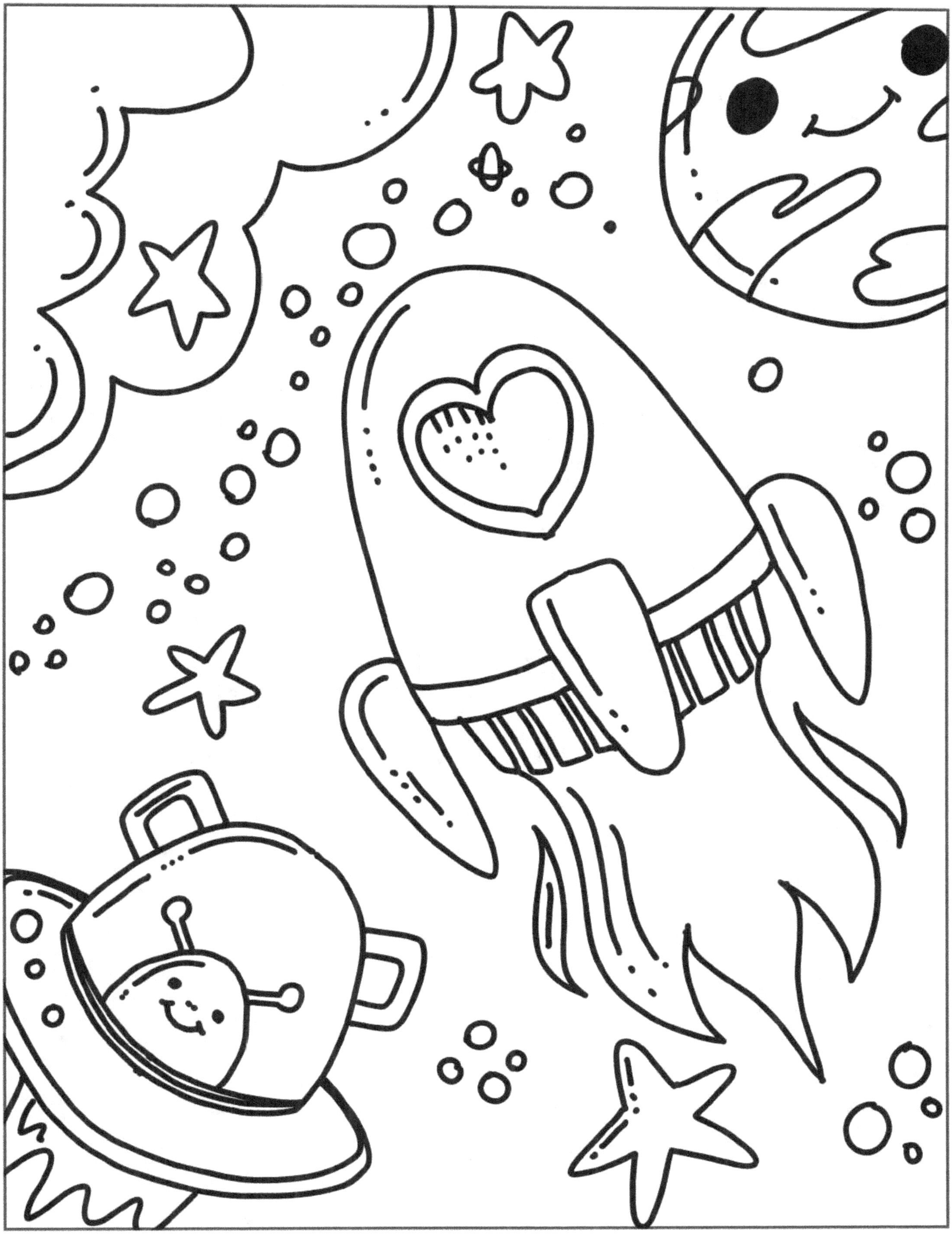

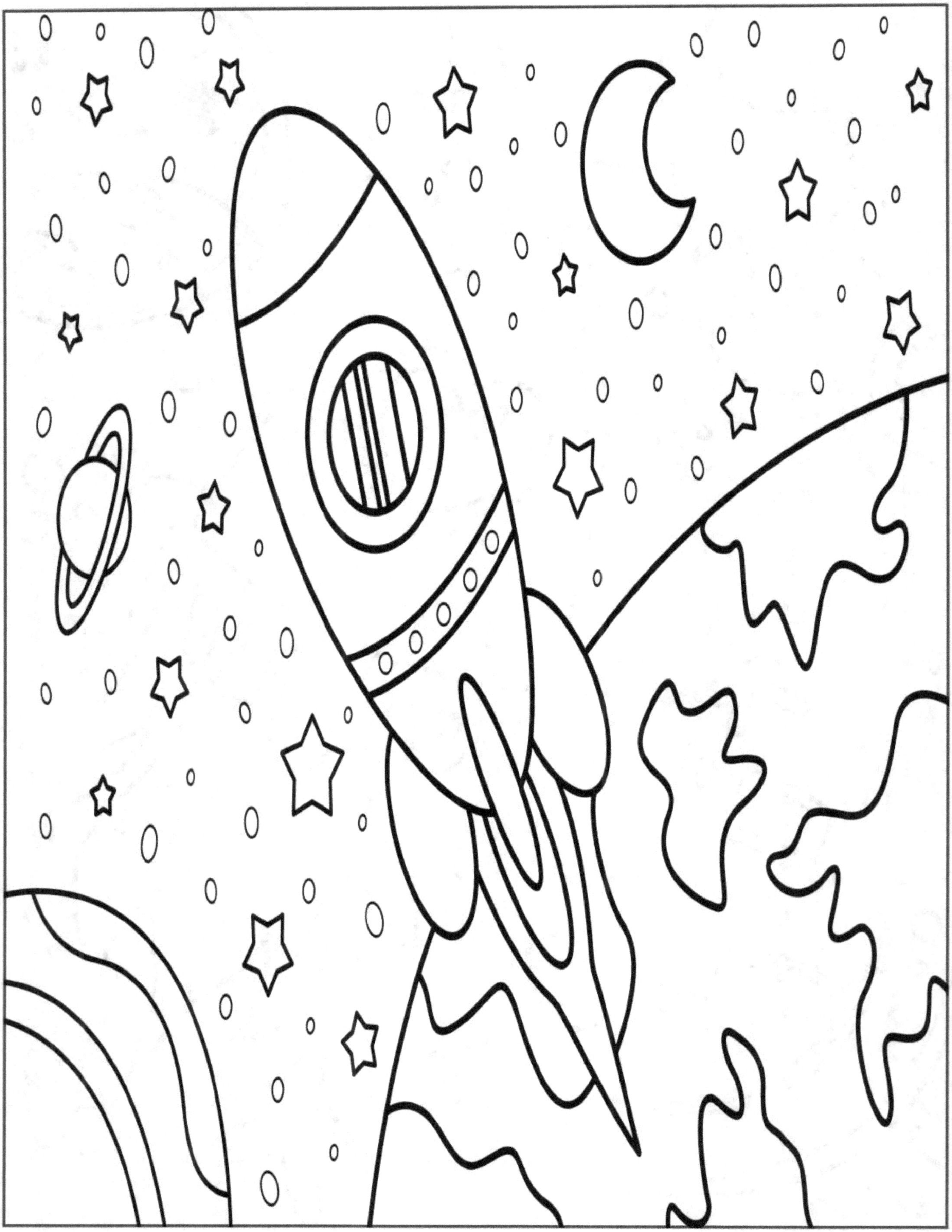

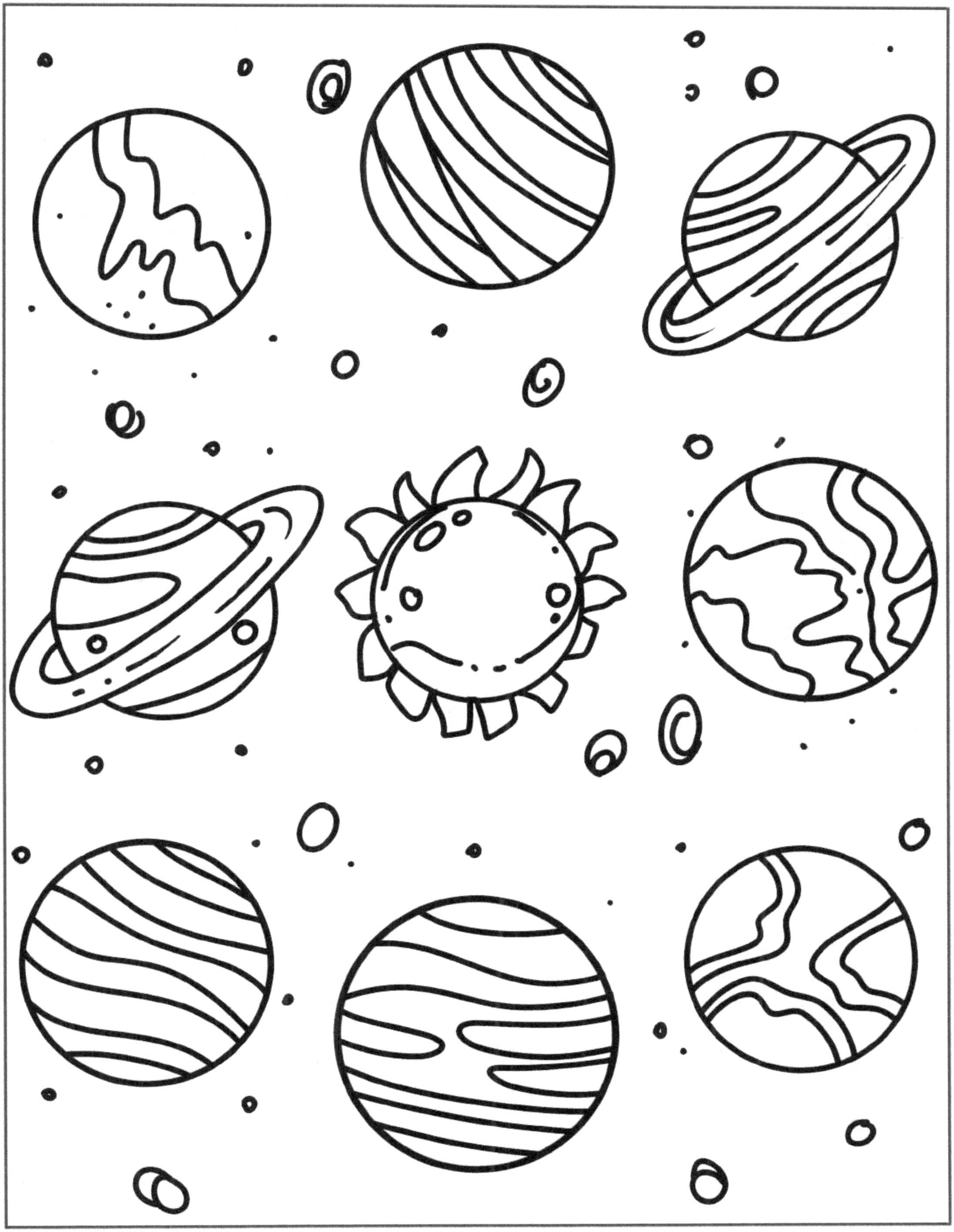

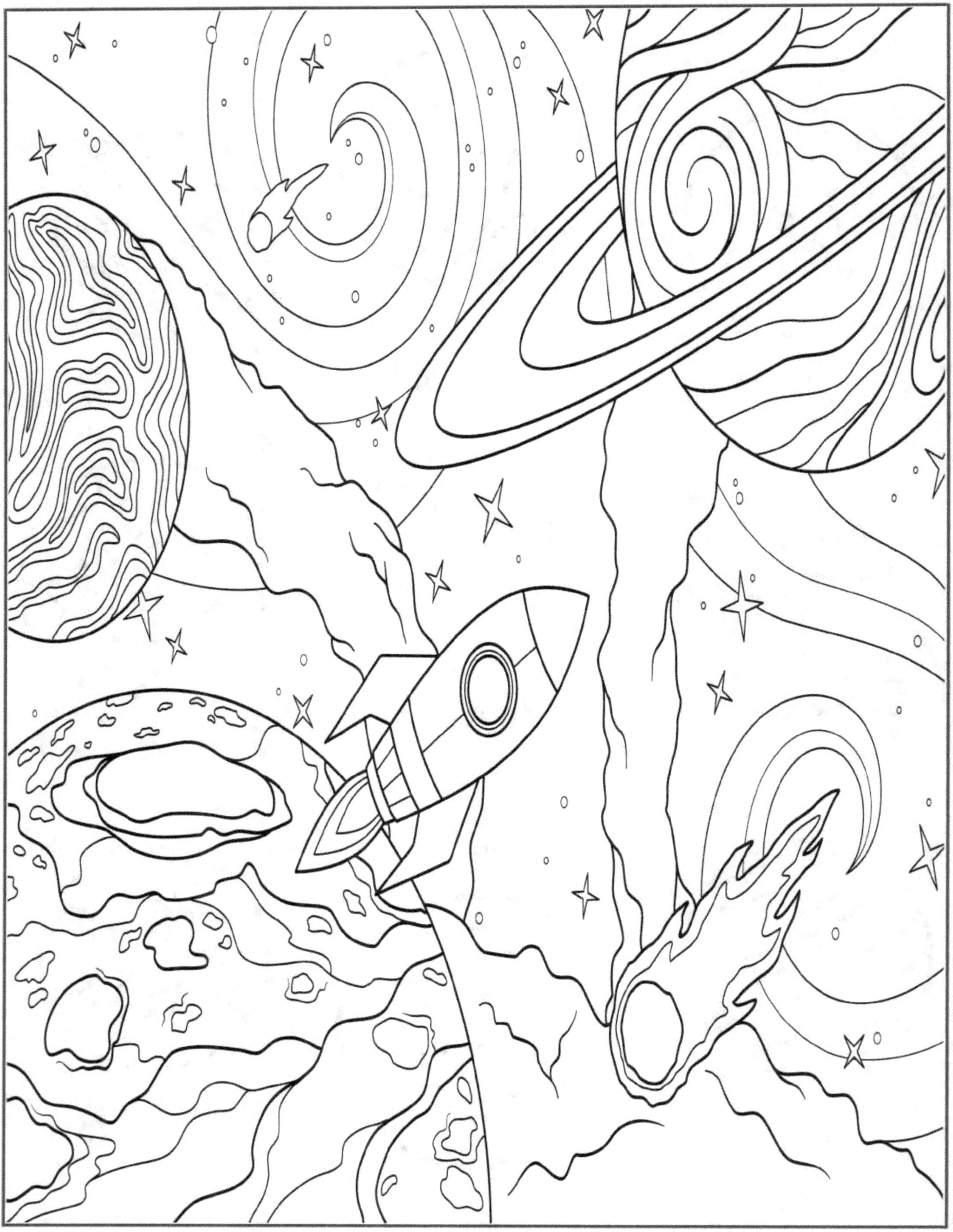

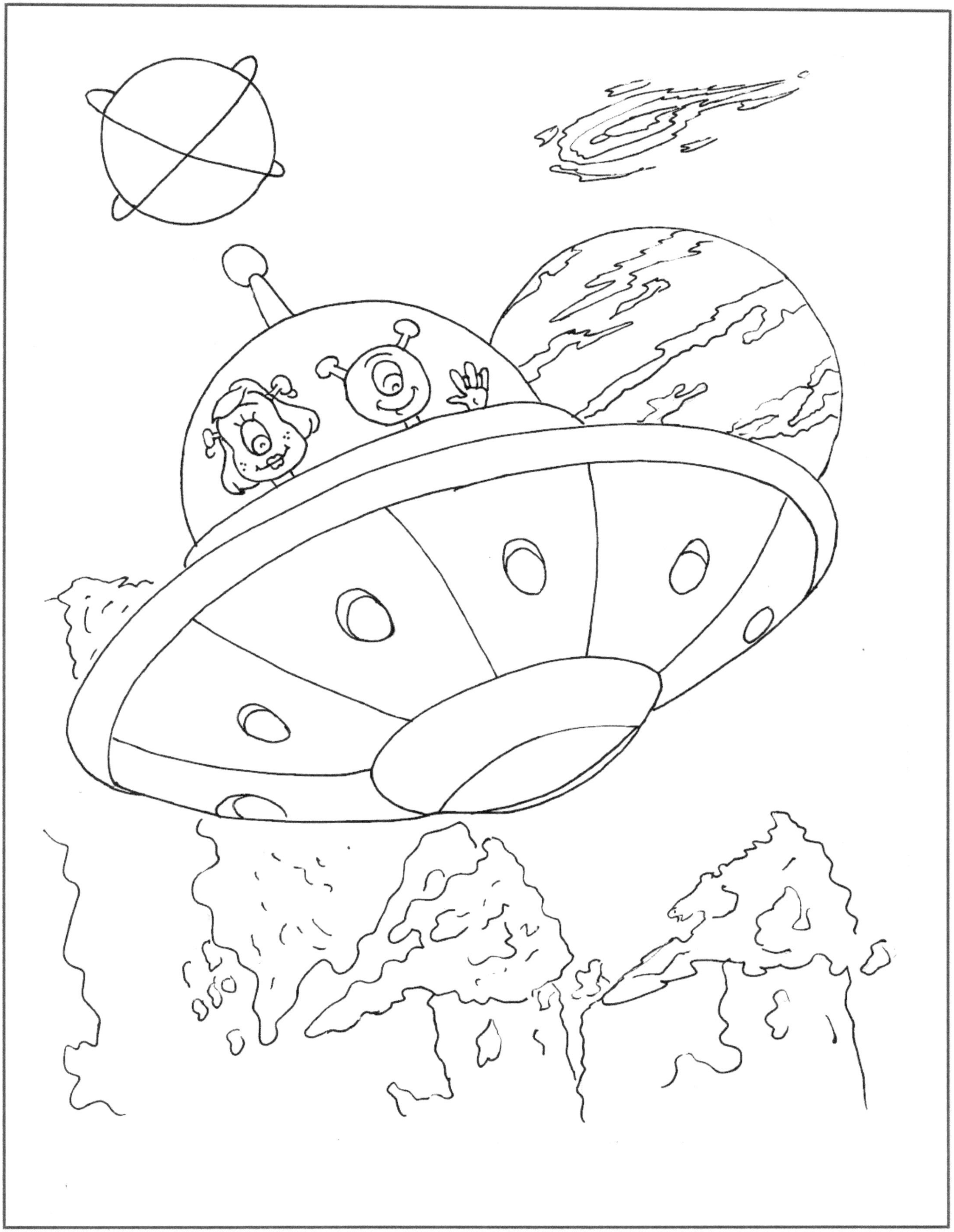

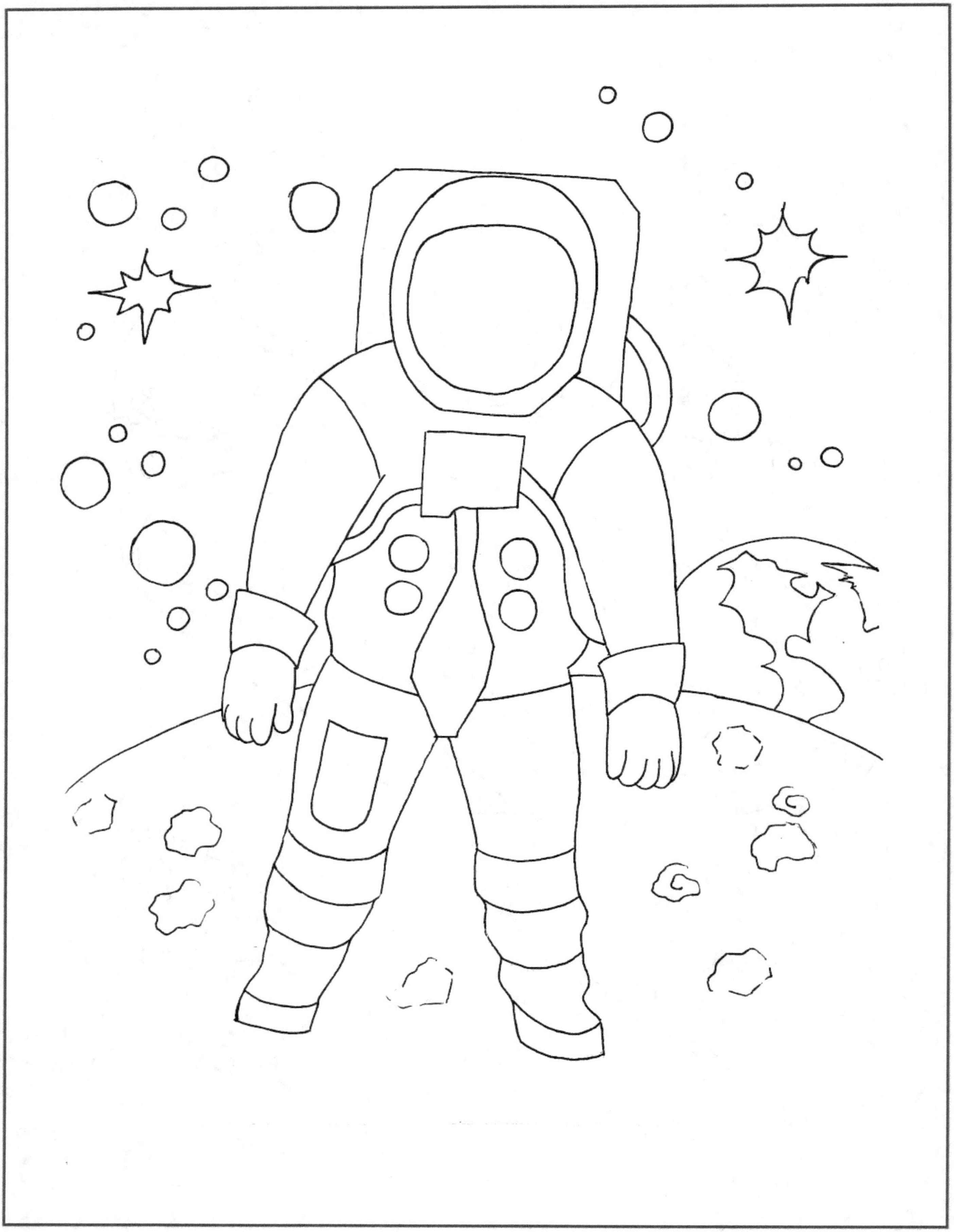

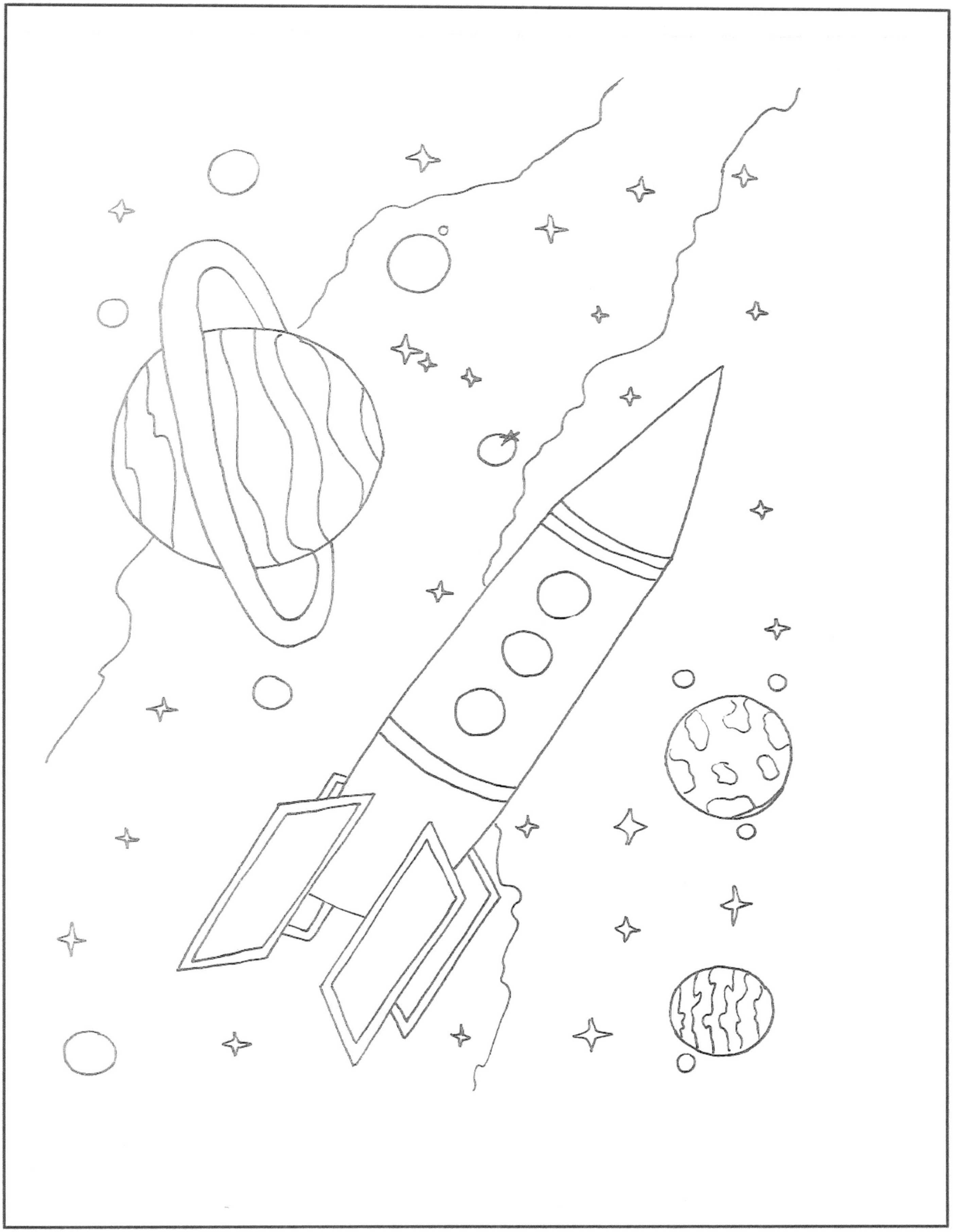

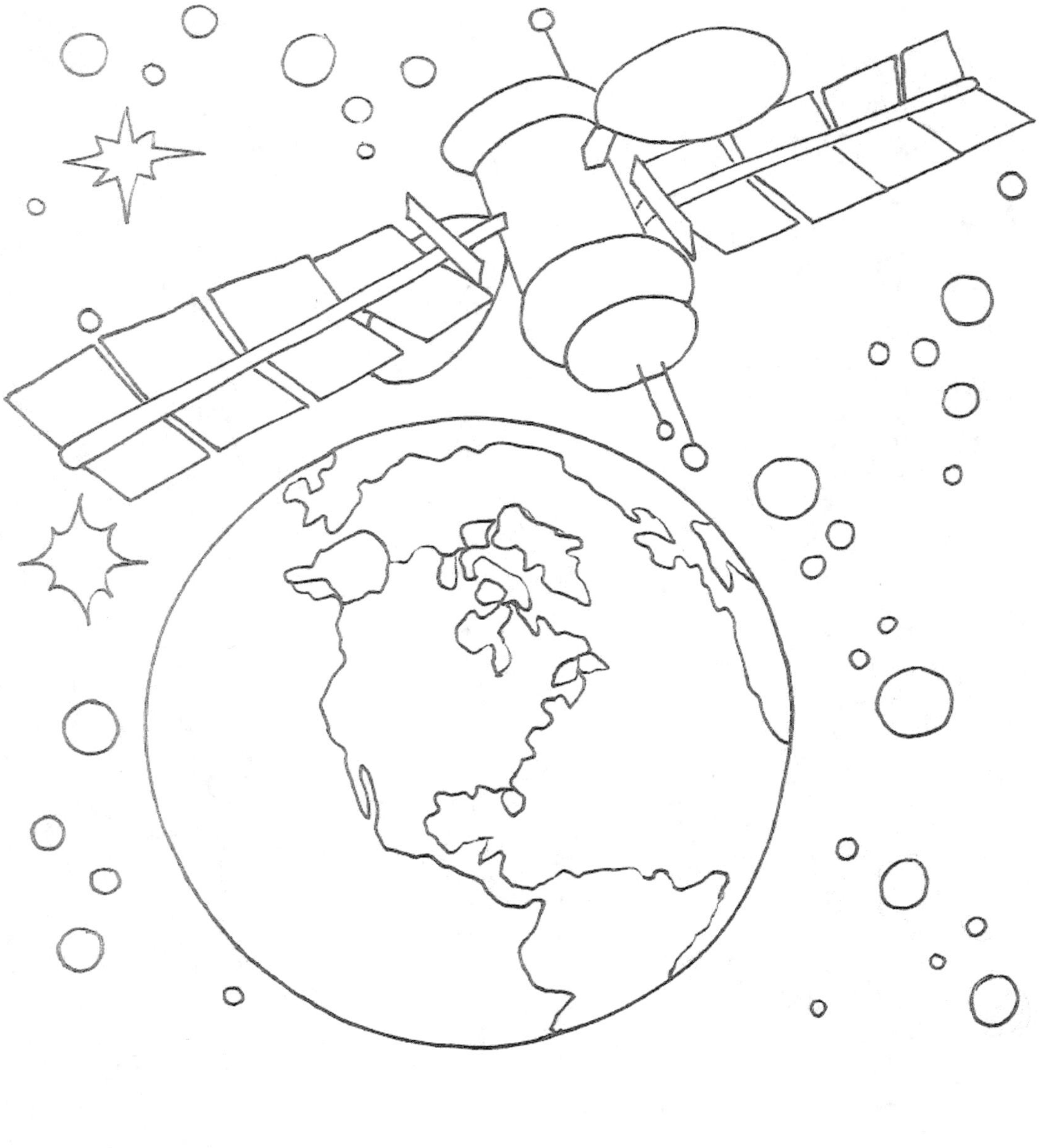

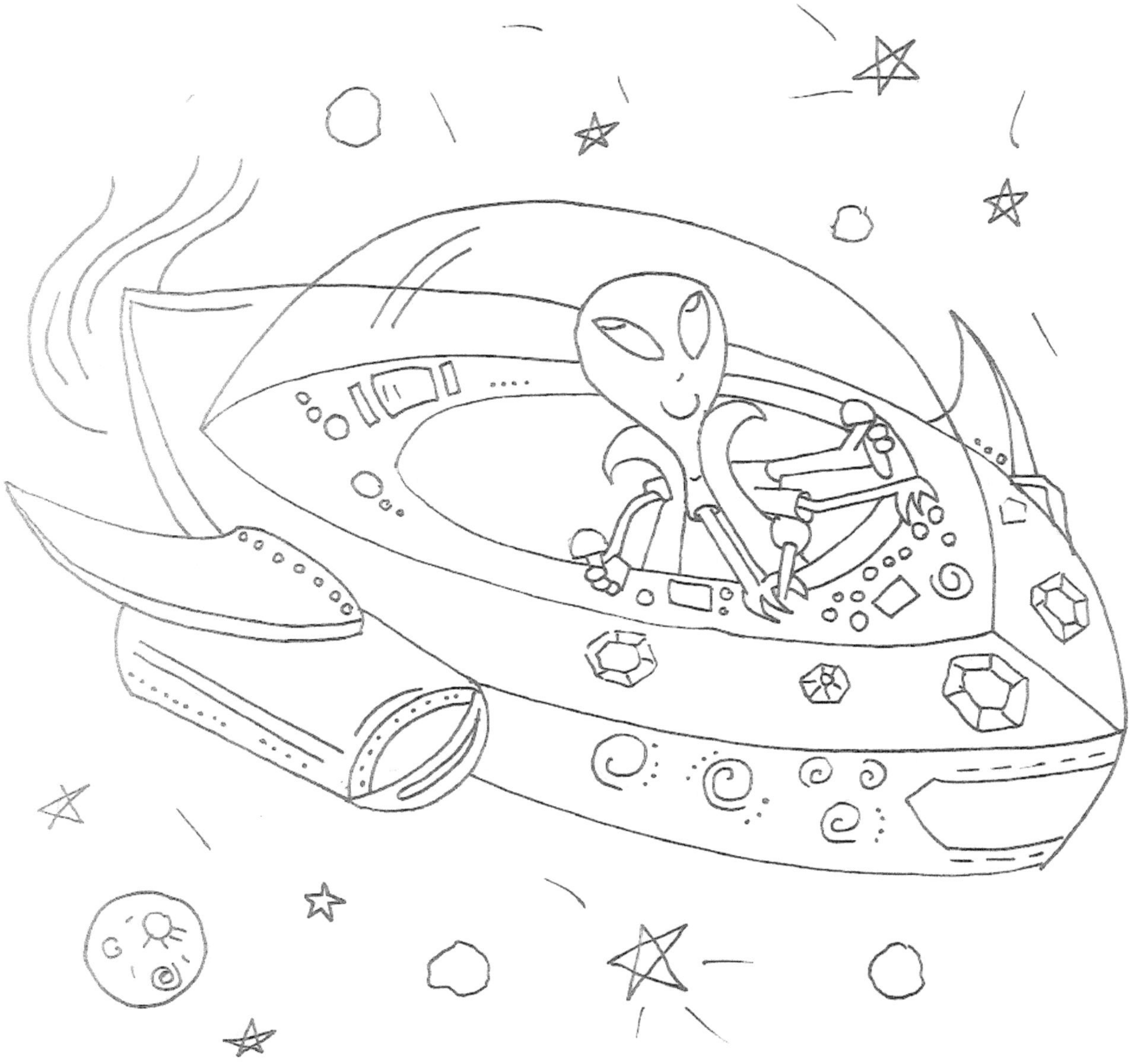

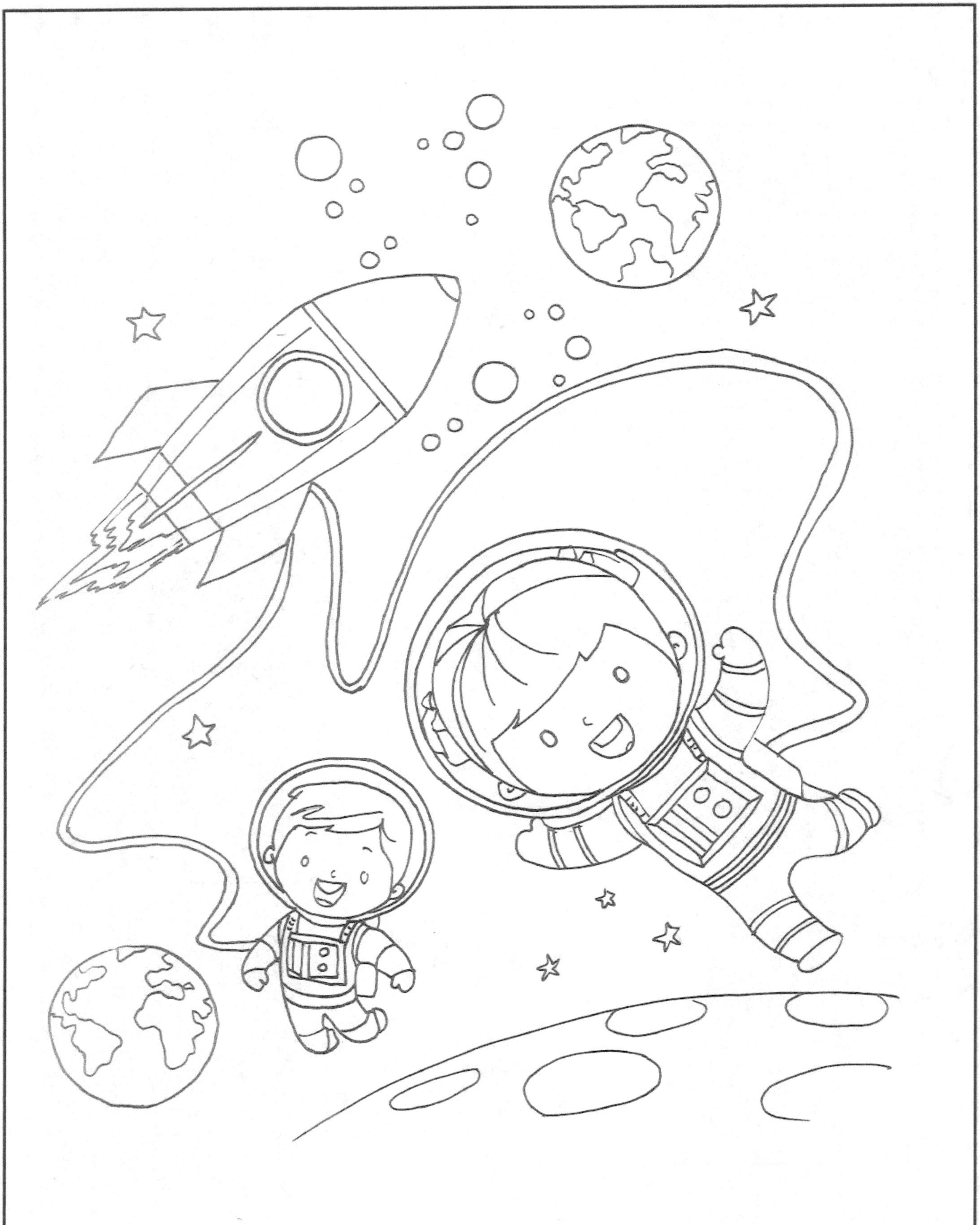

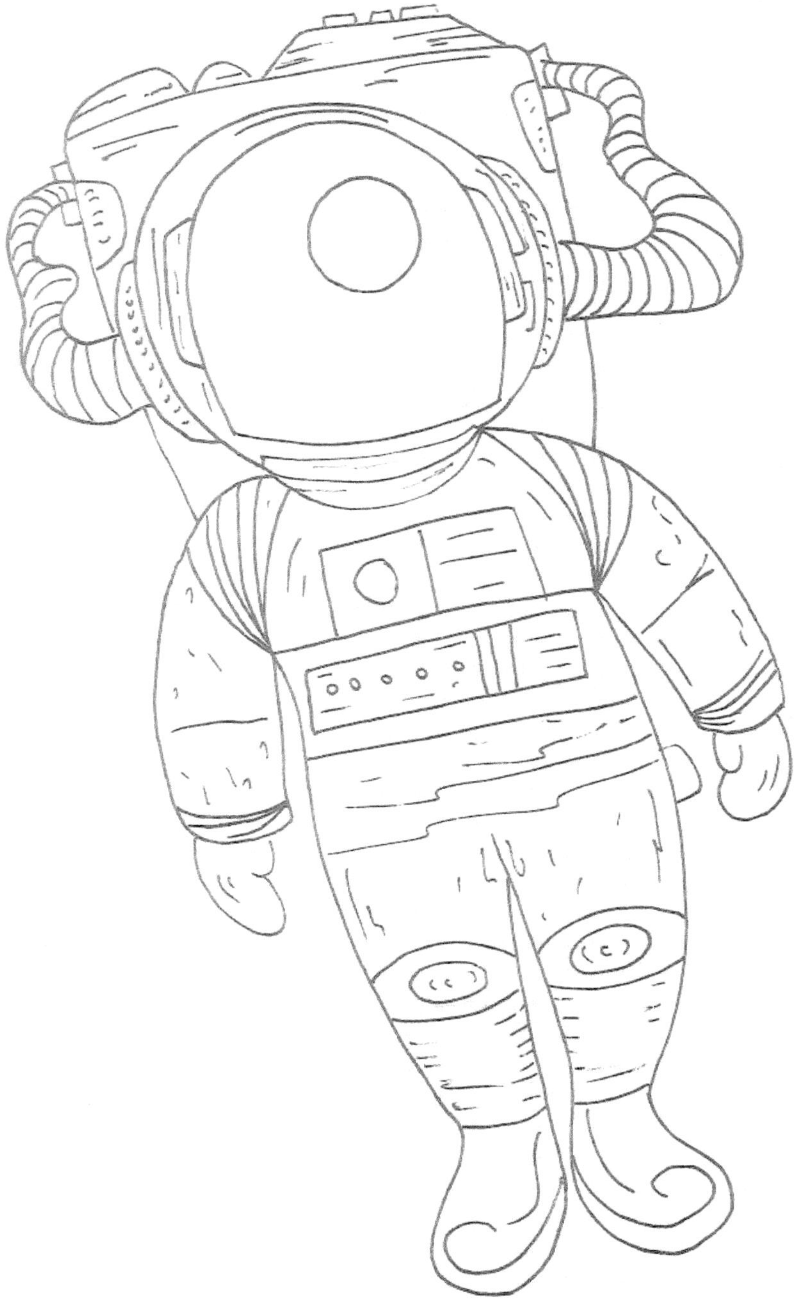

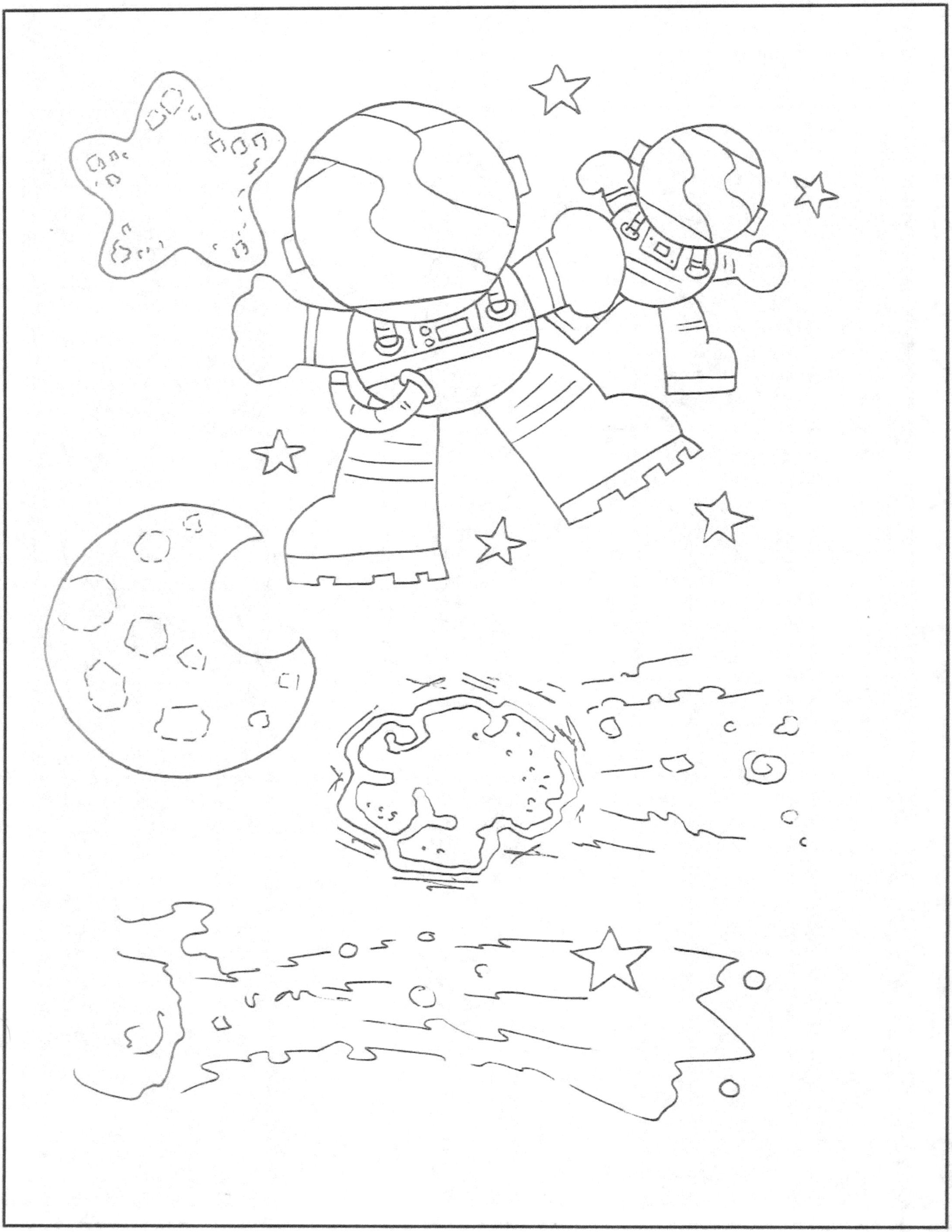

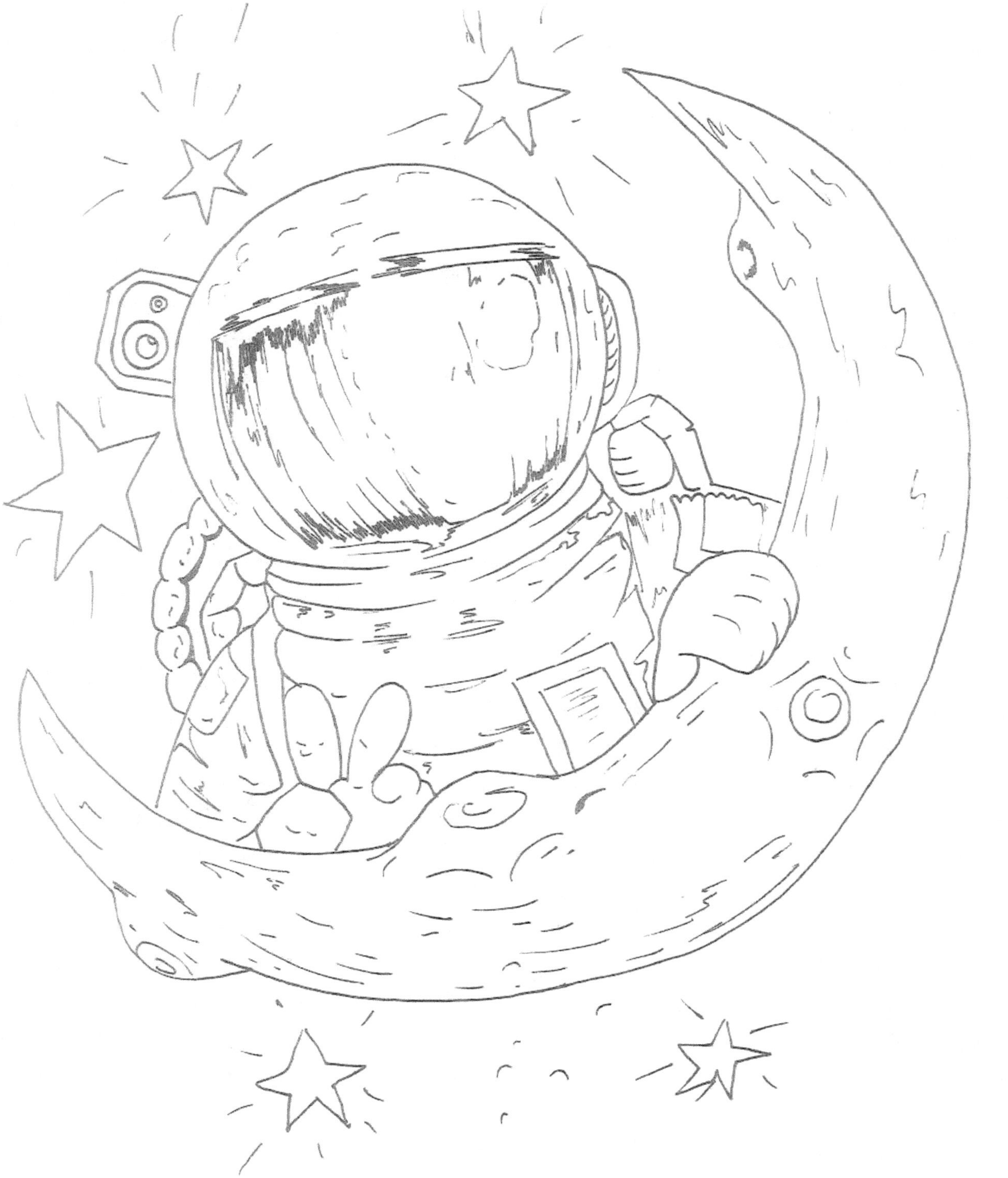

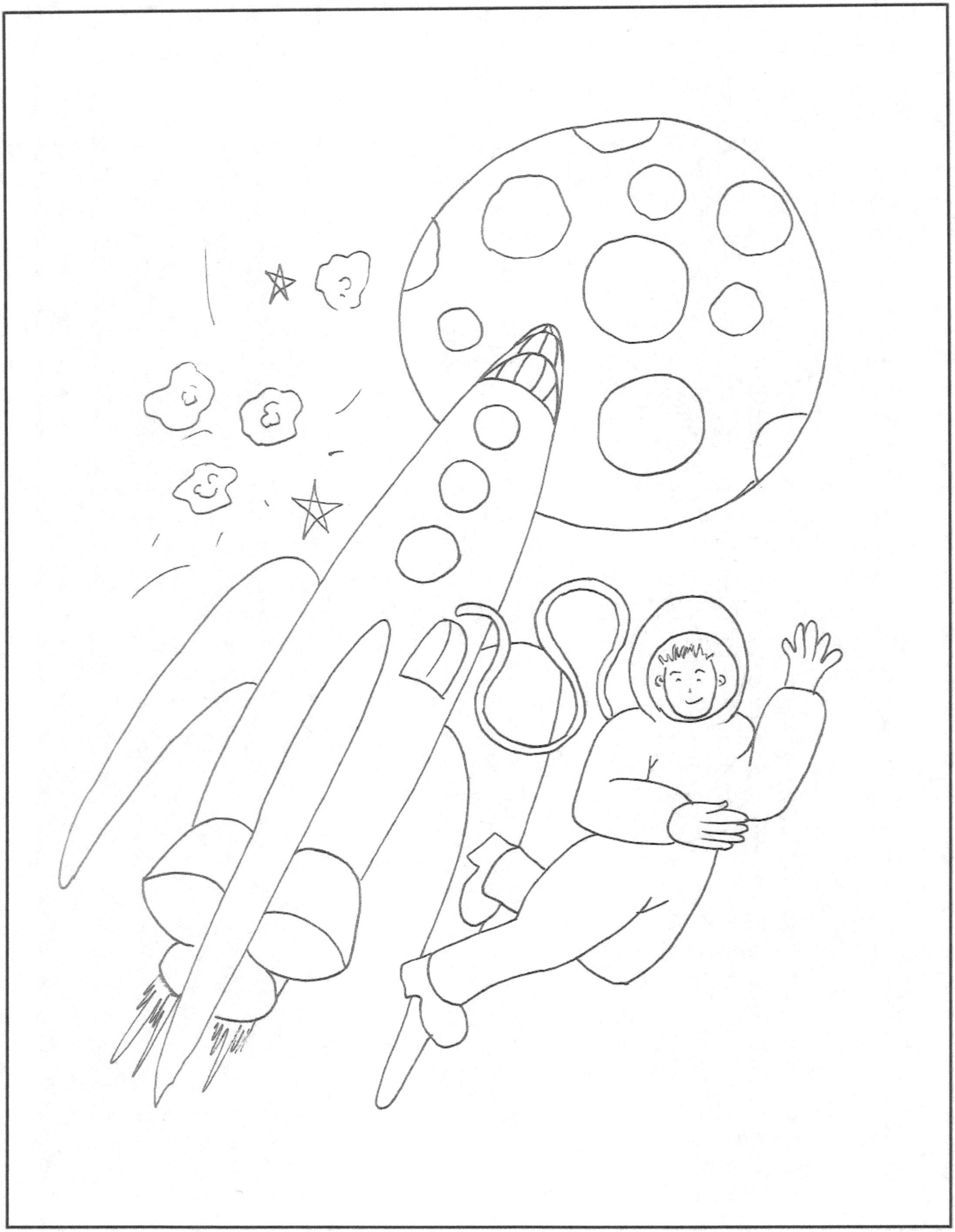

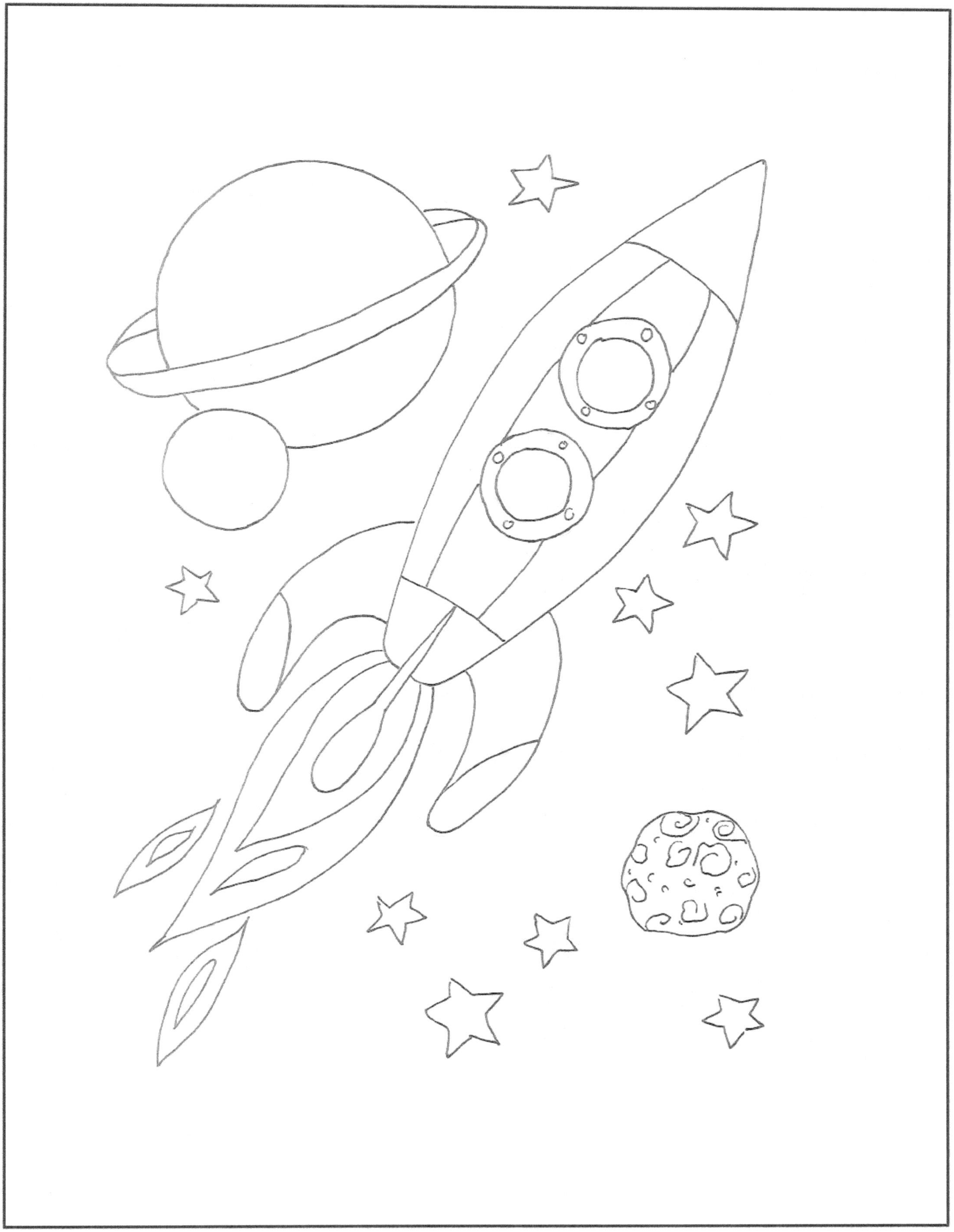

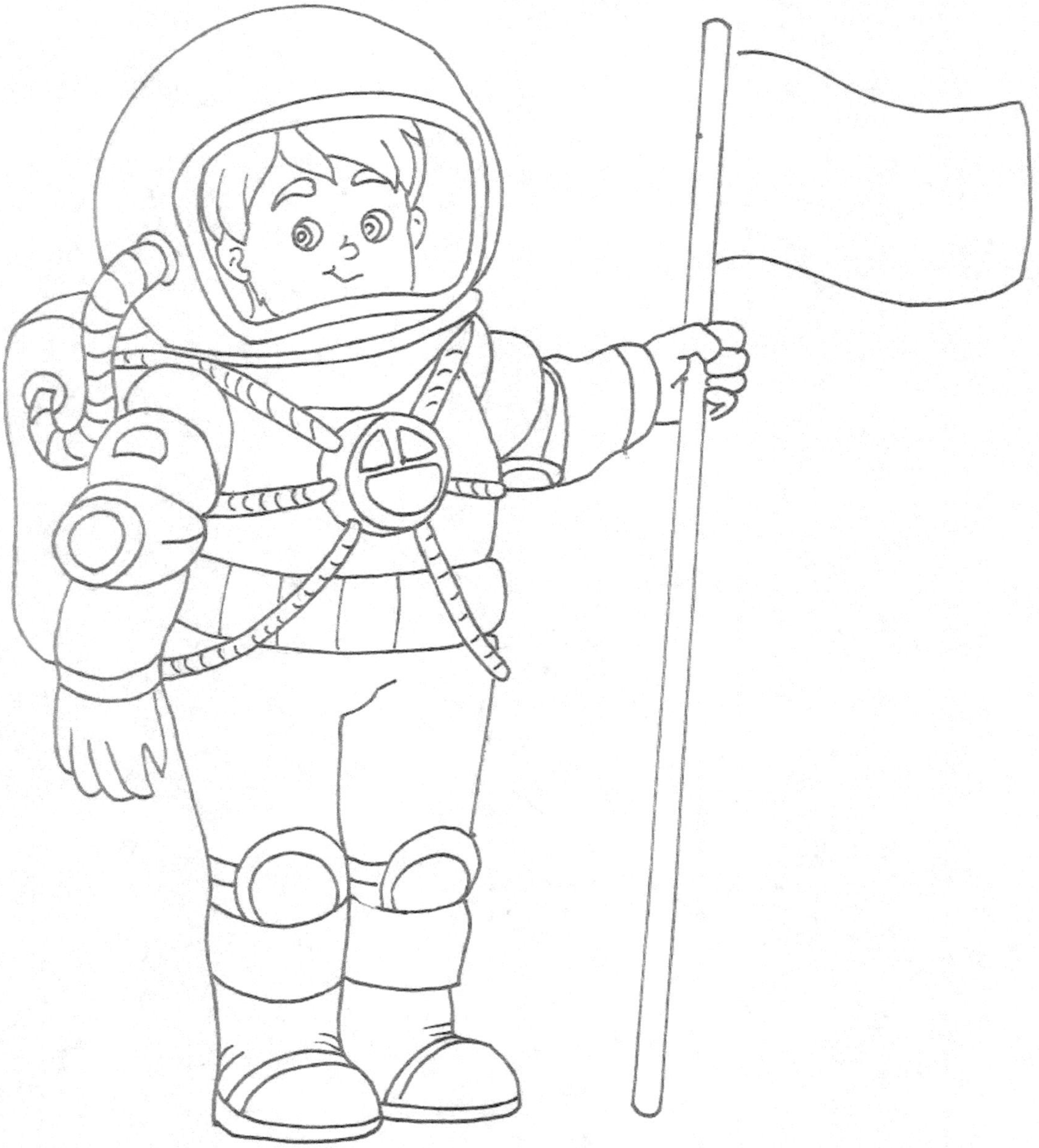

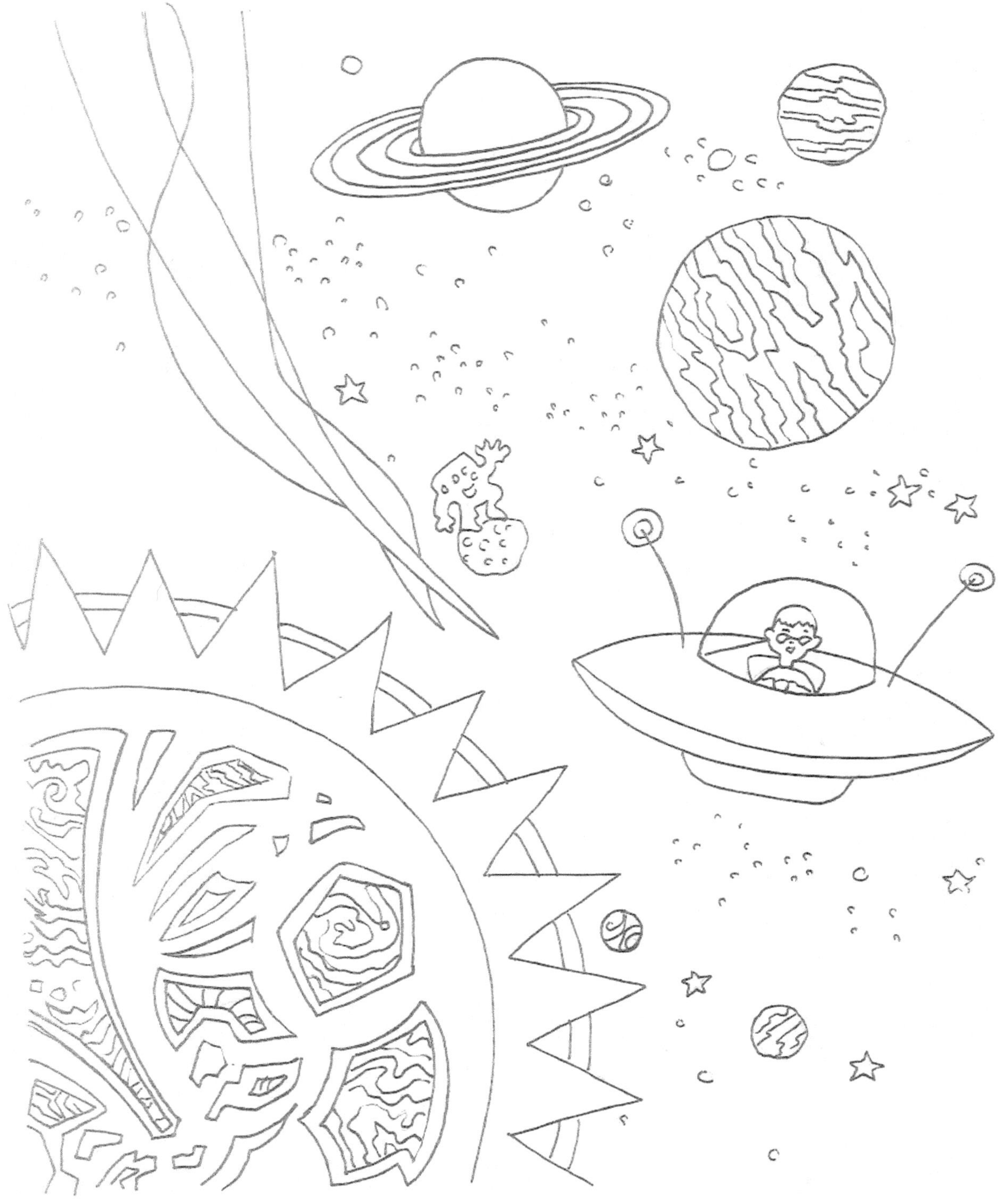

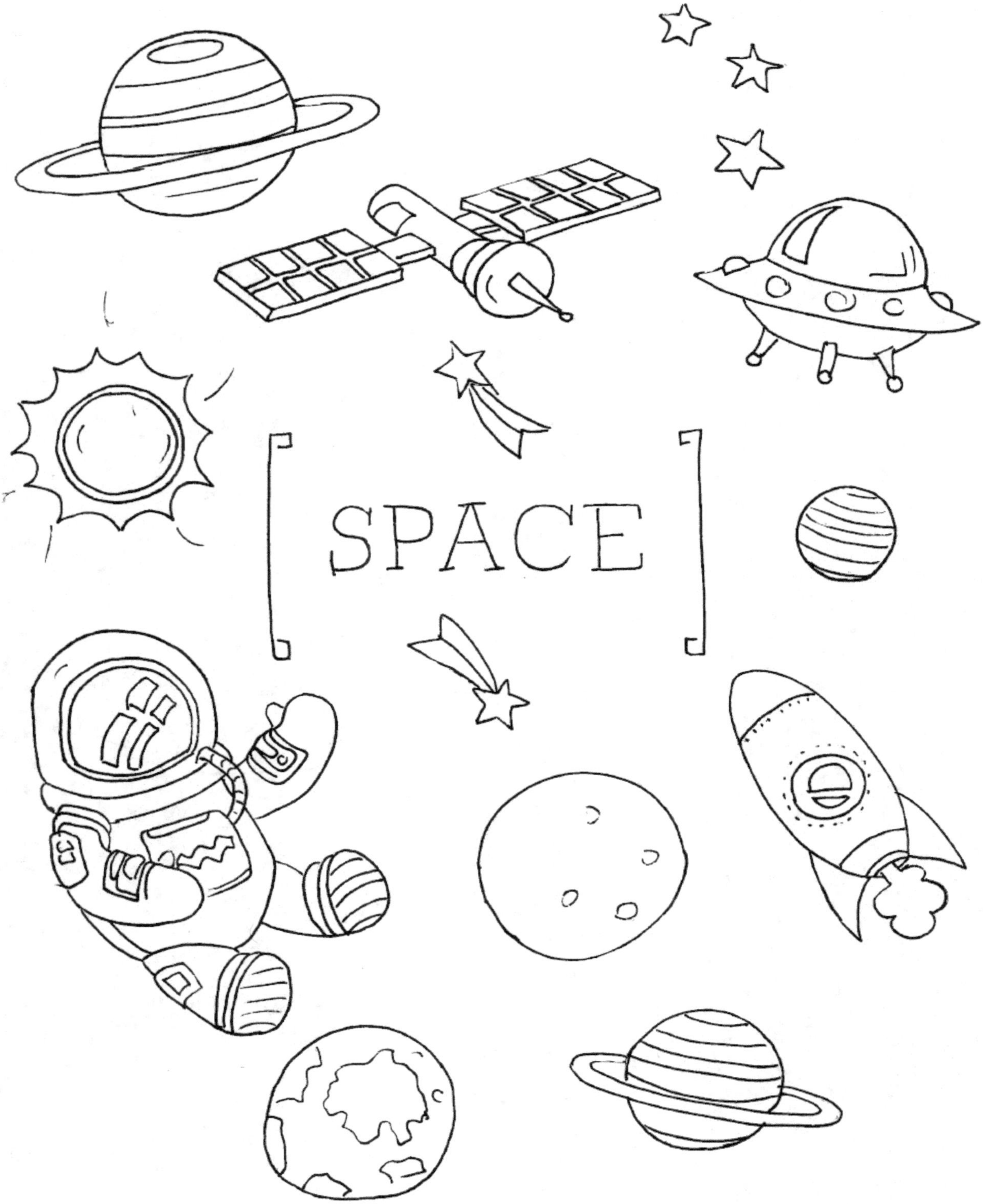
SPACE

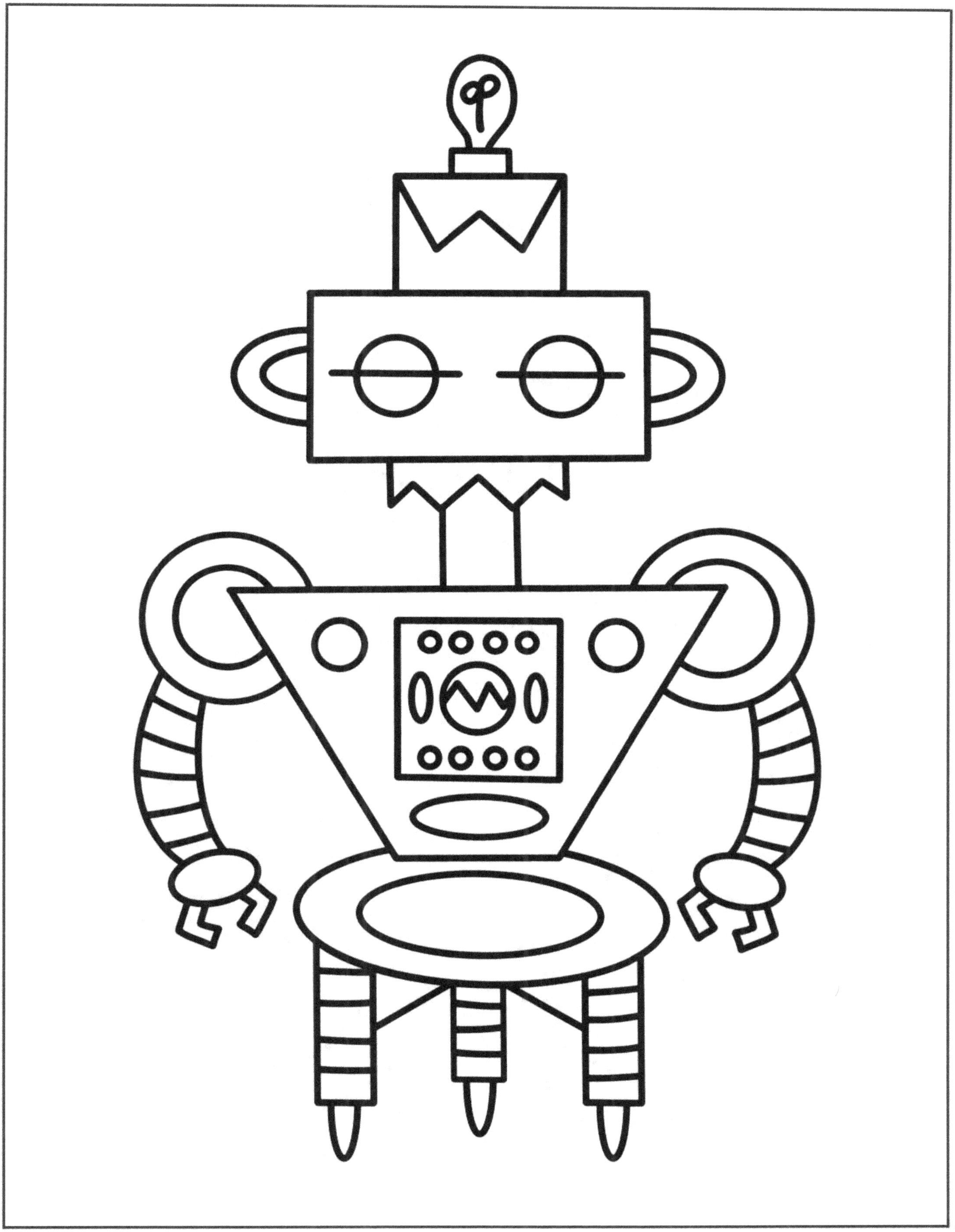

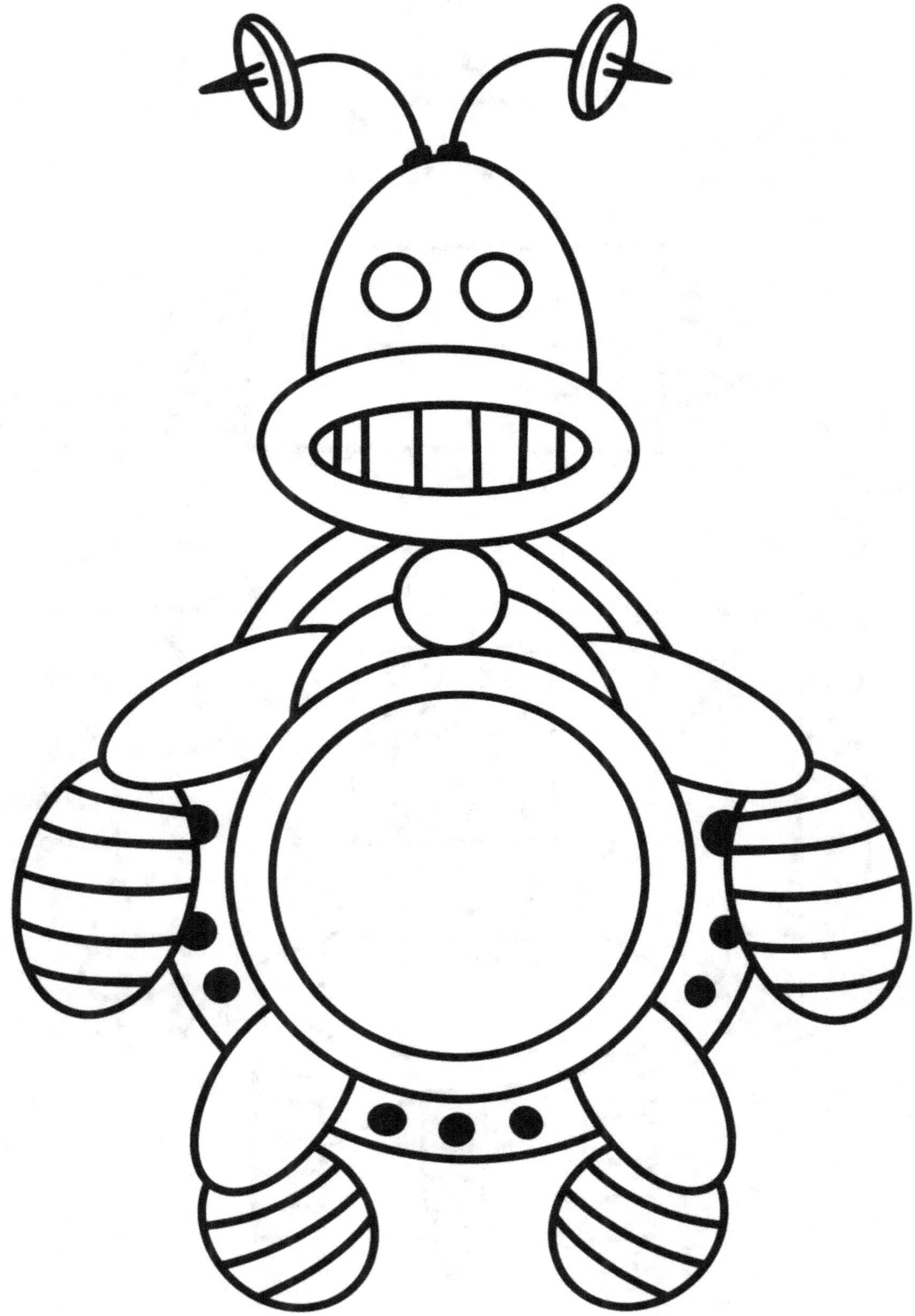

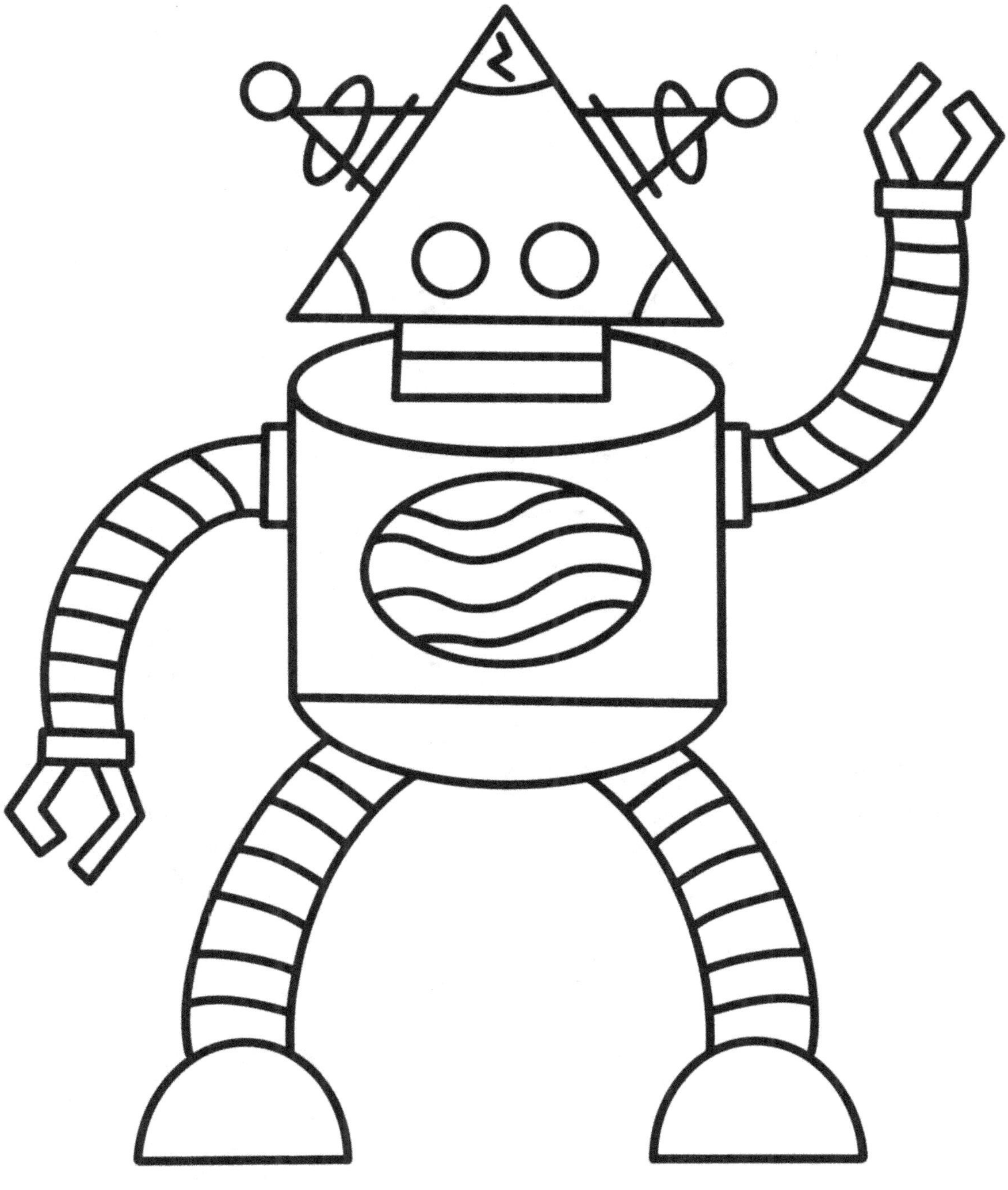

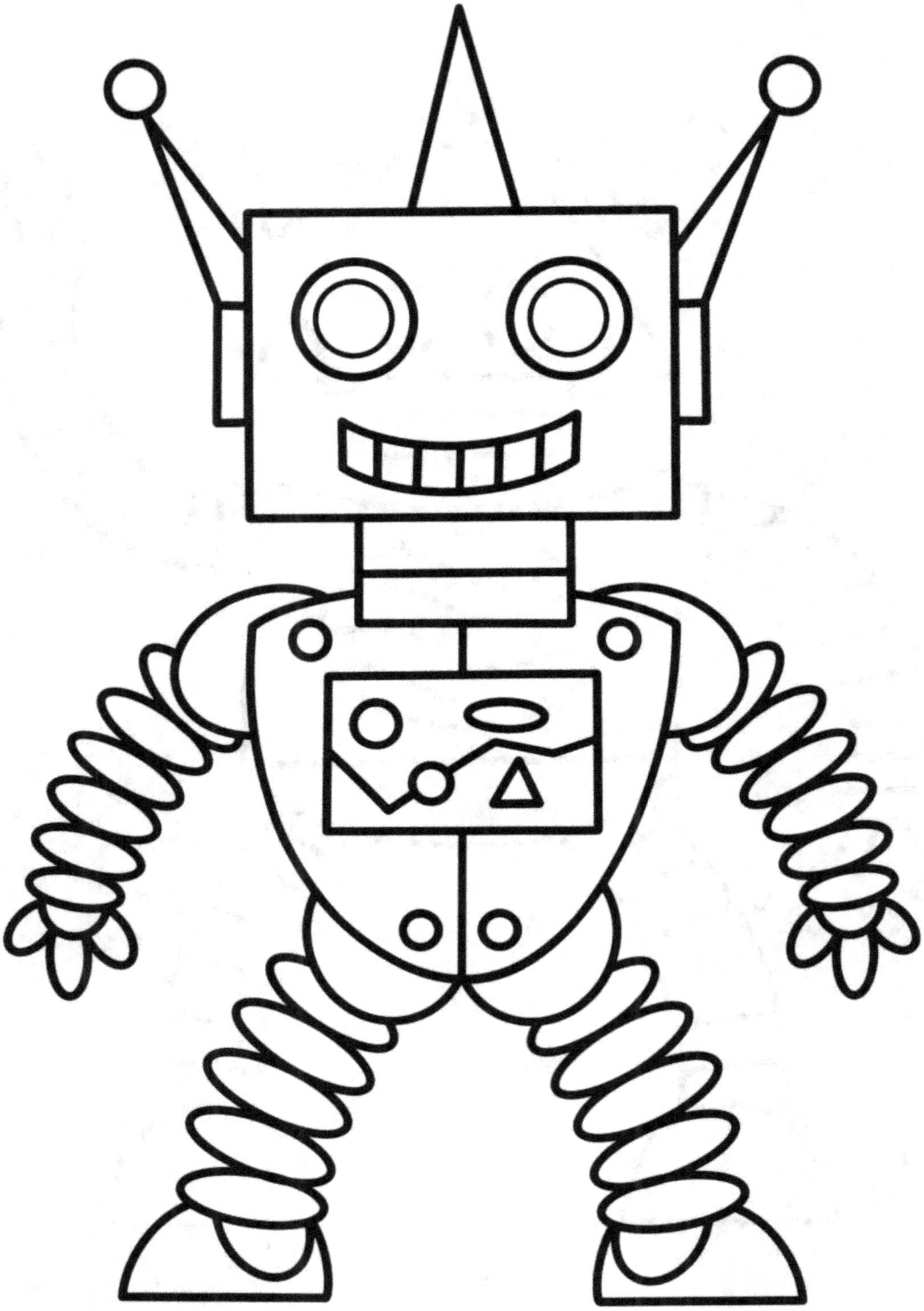

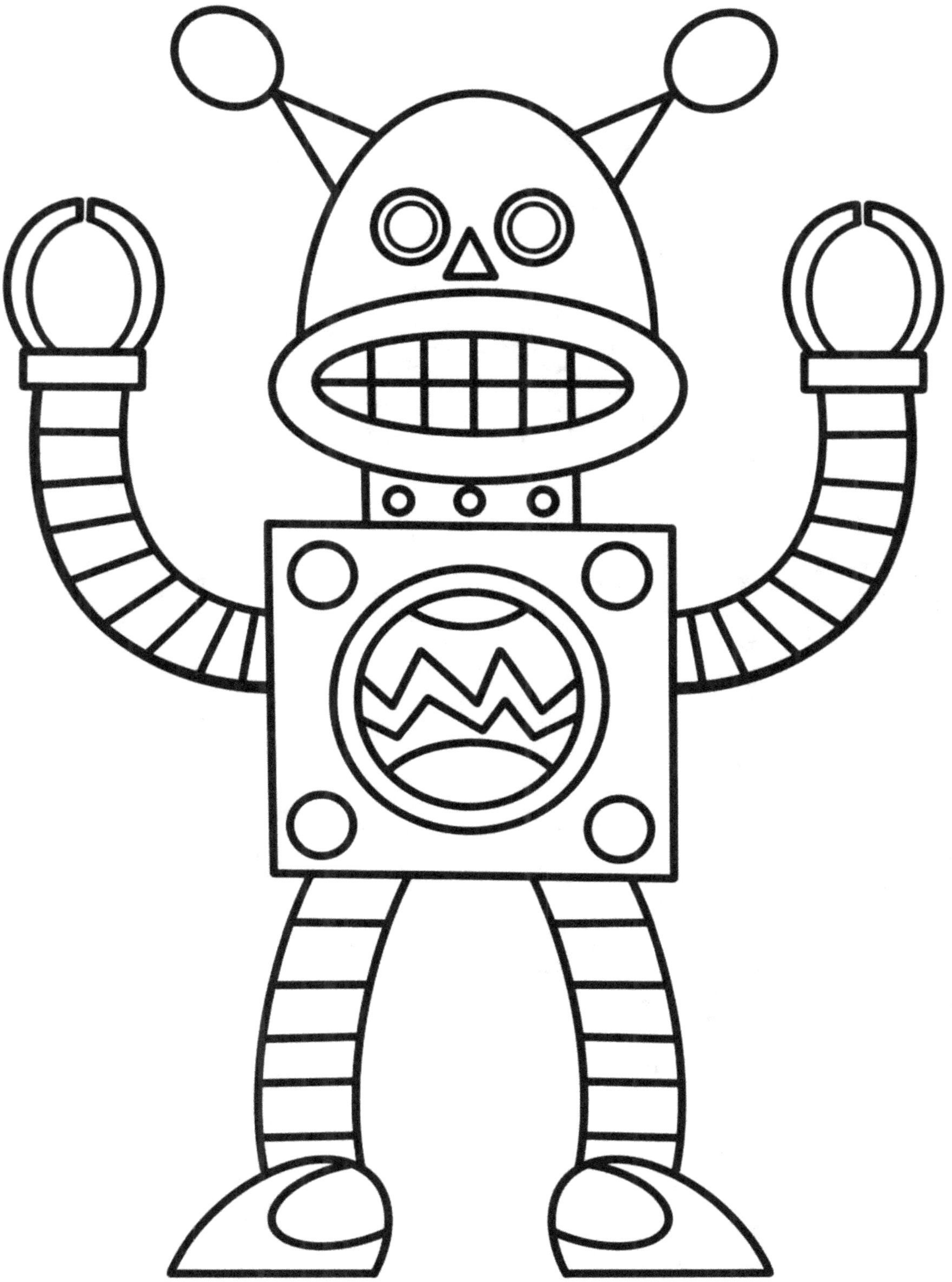

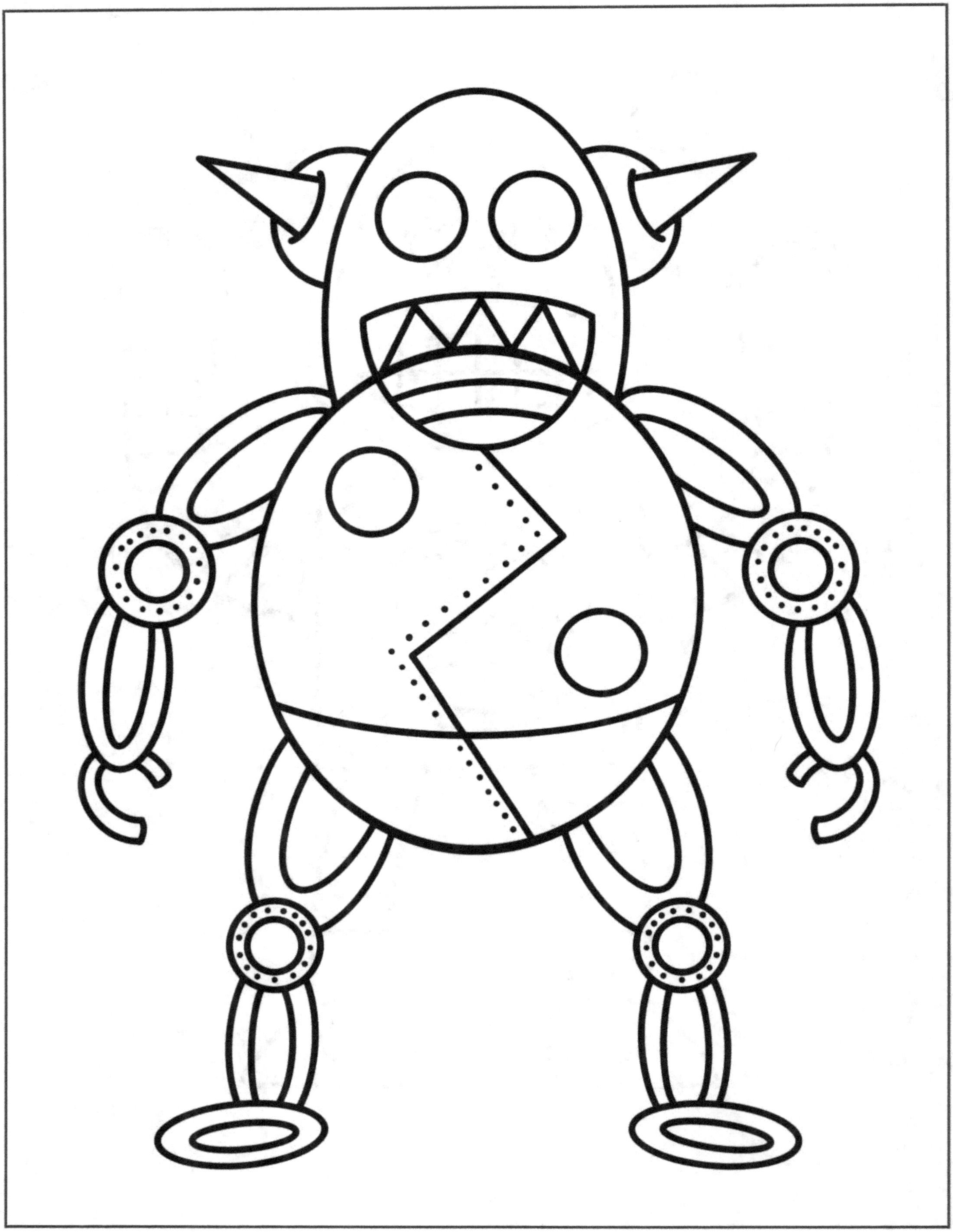

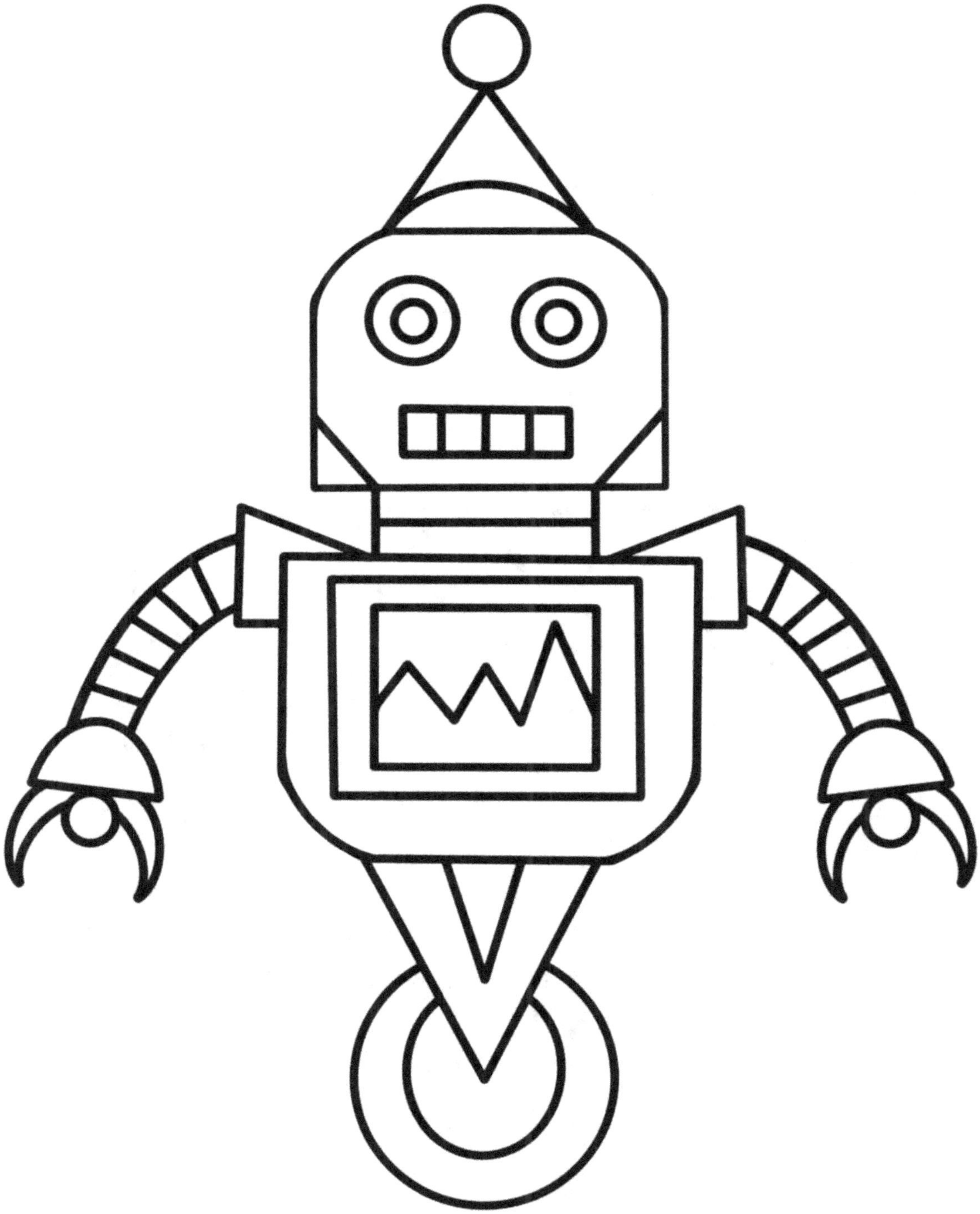

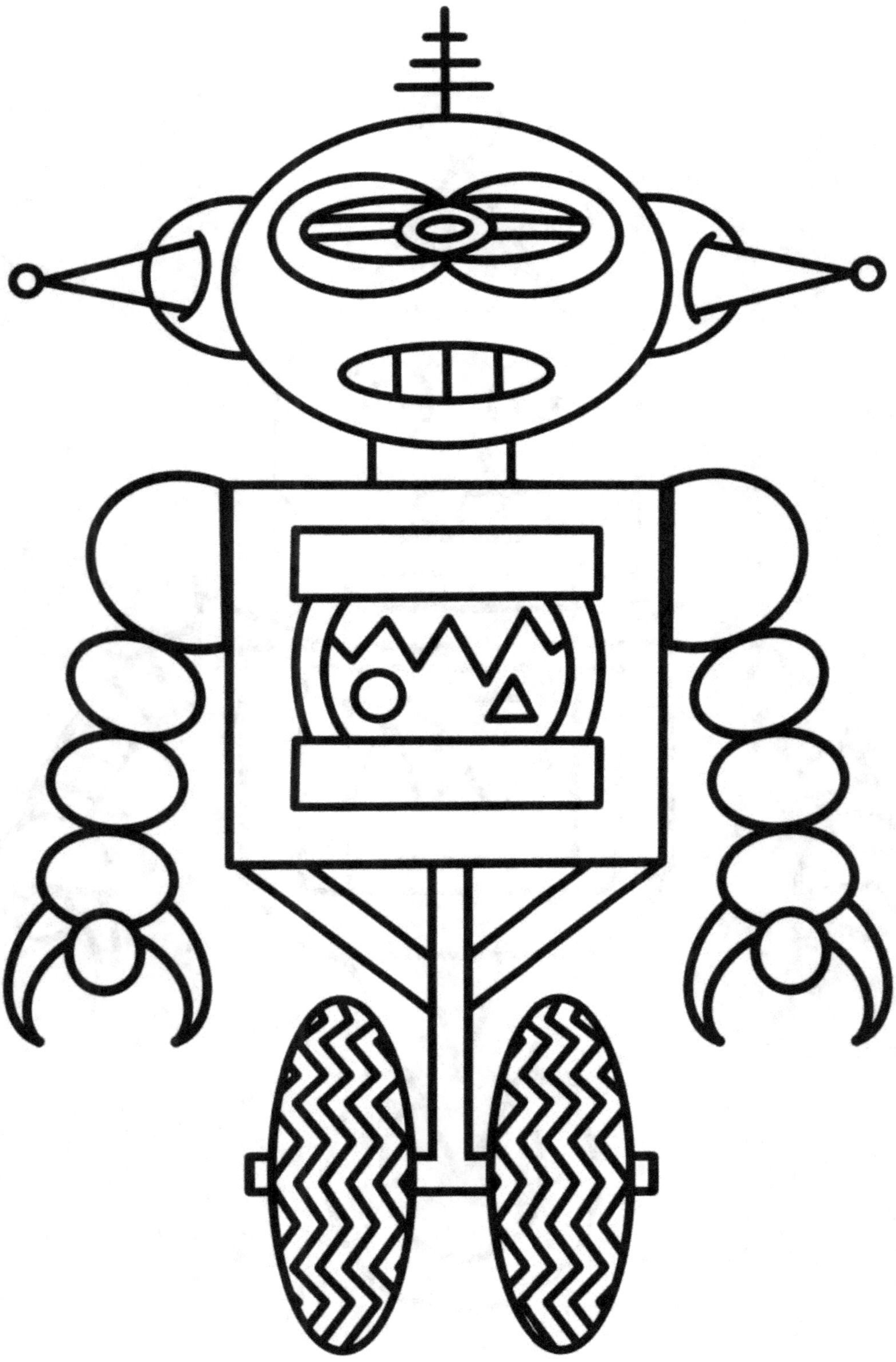

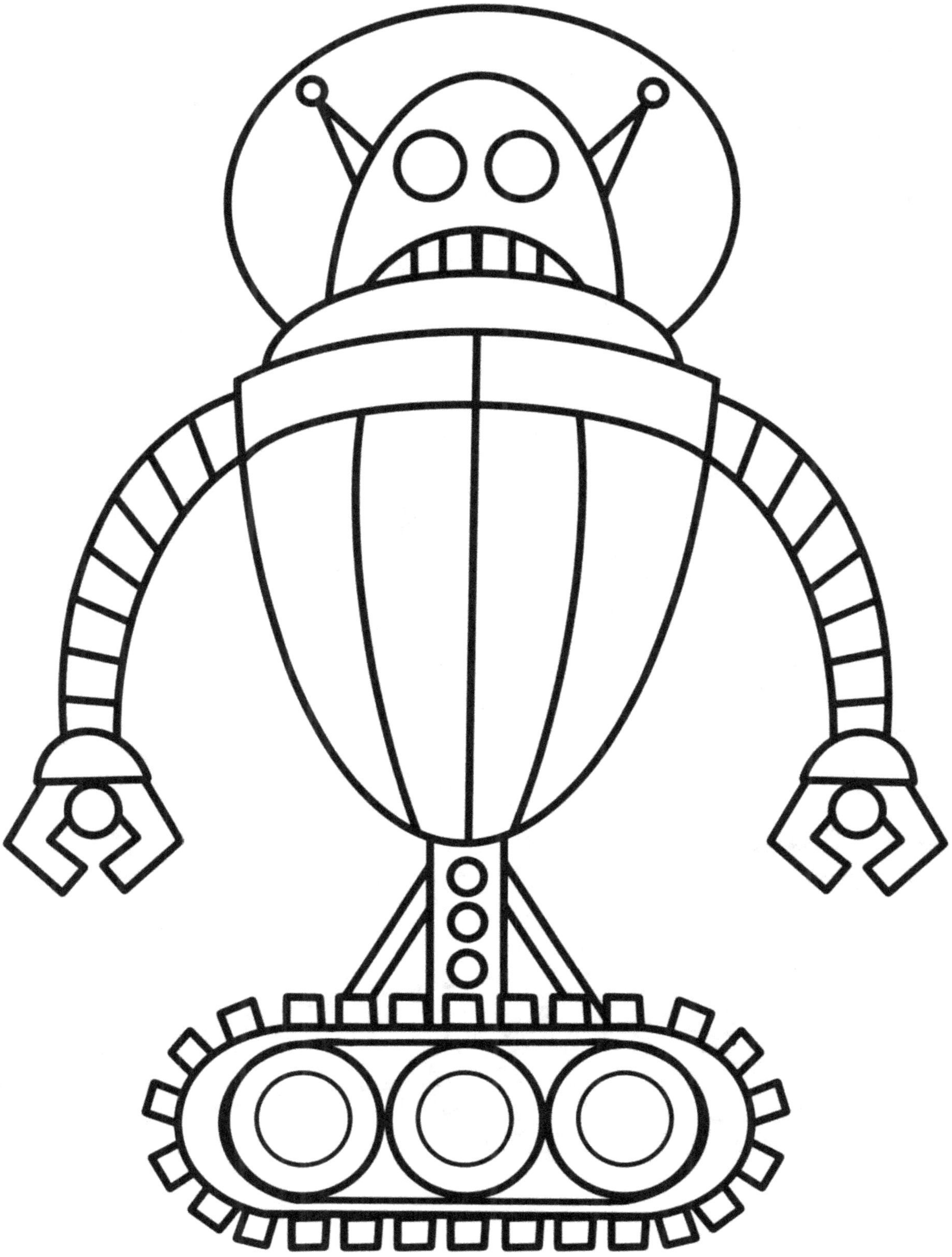

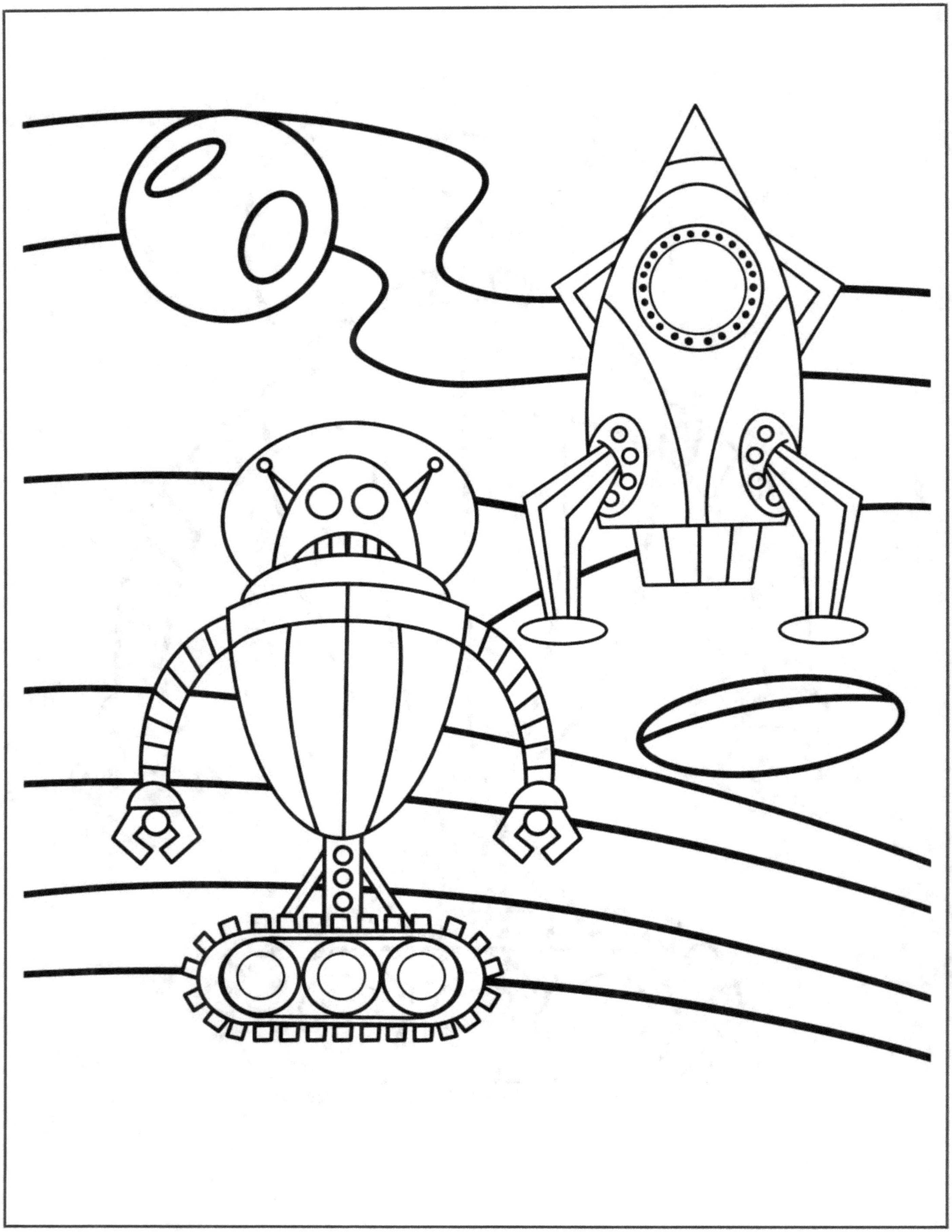

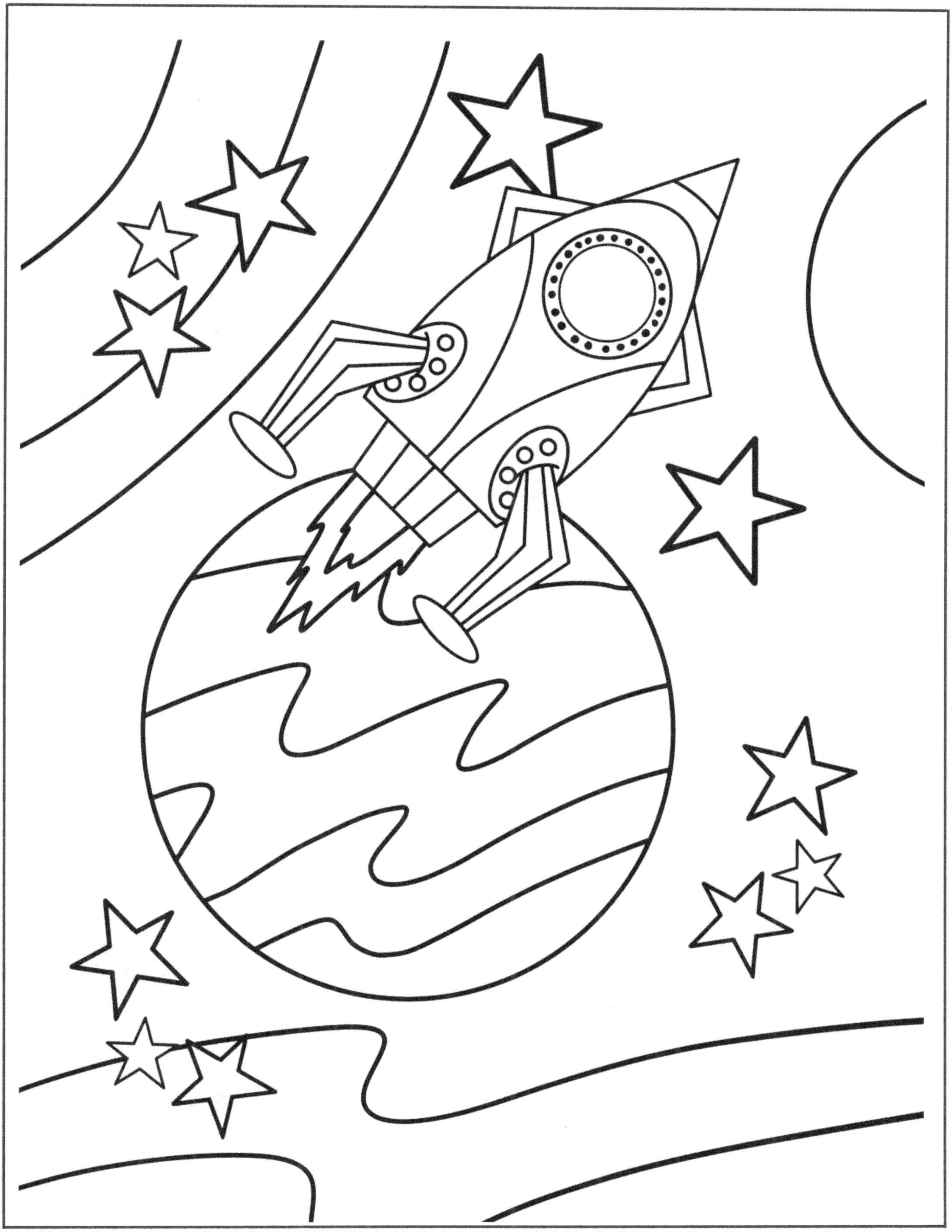

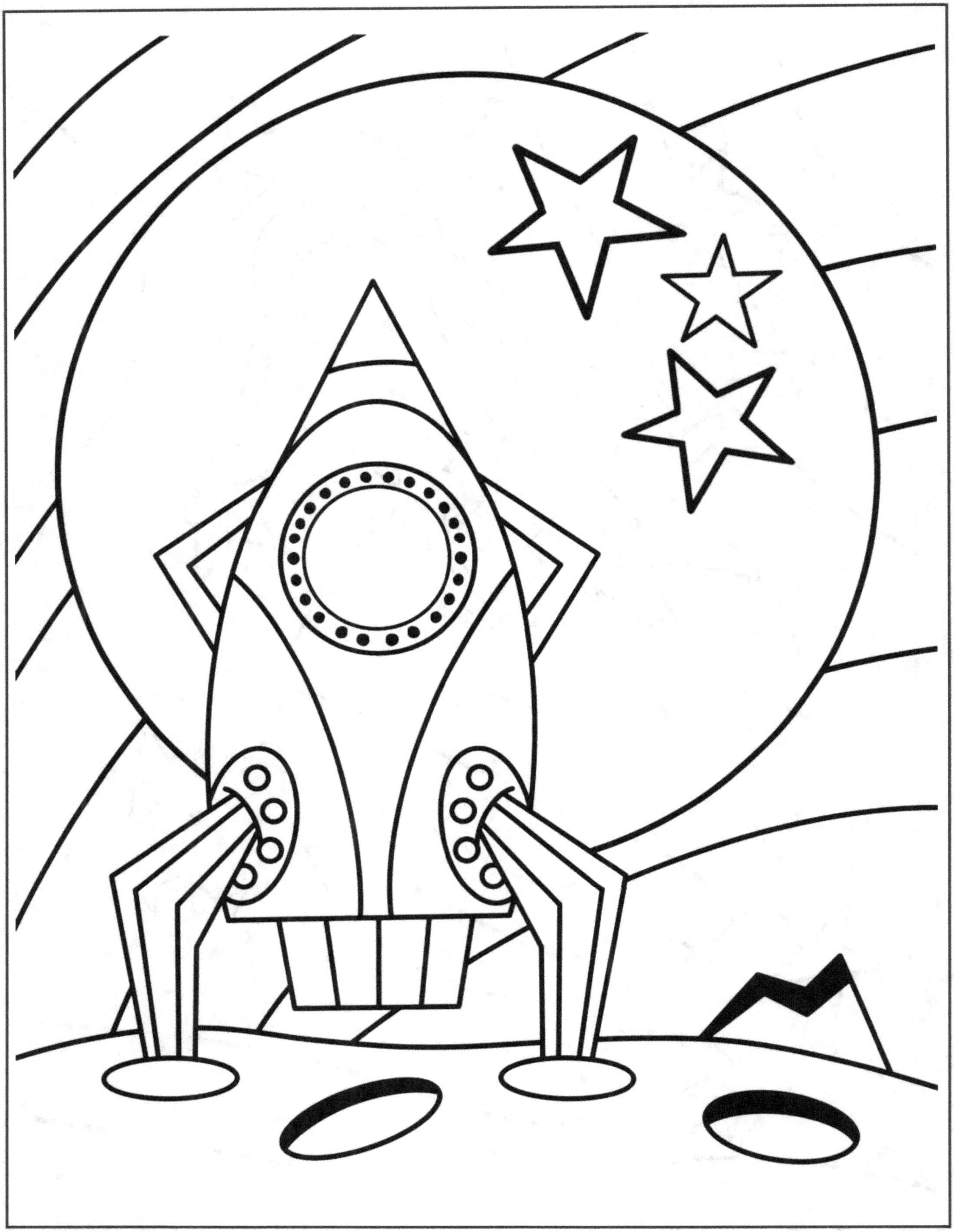

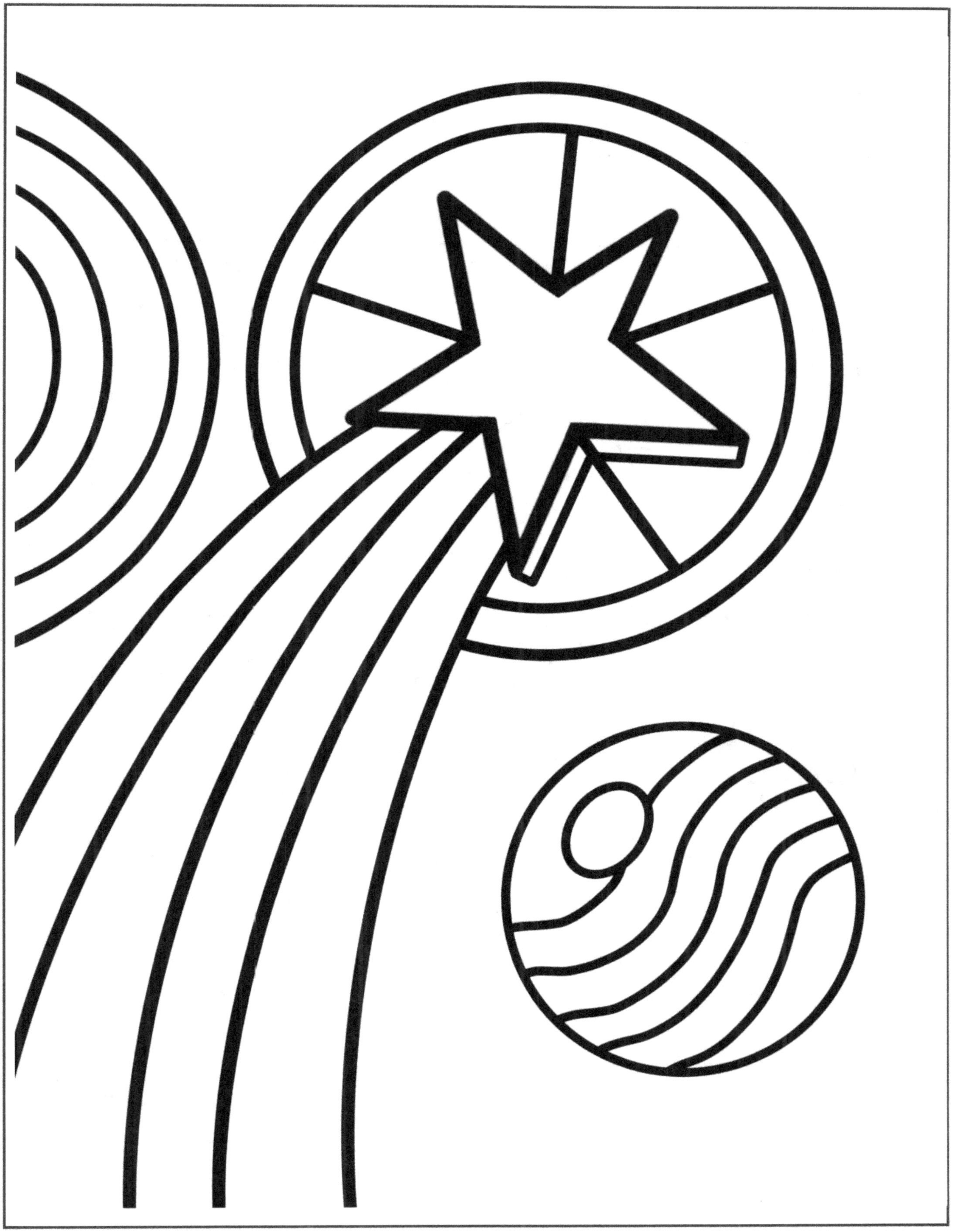

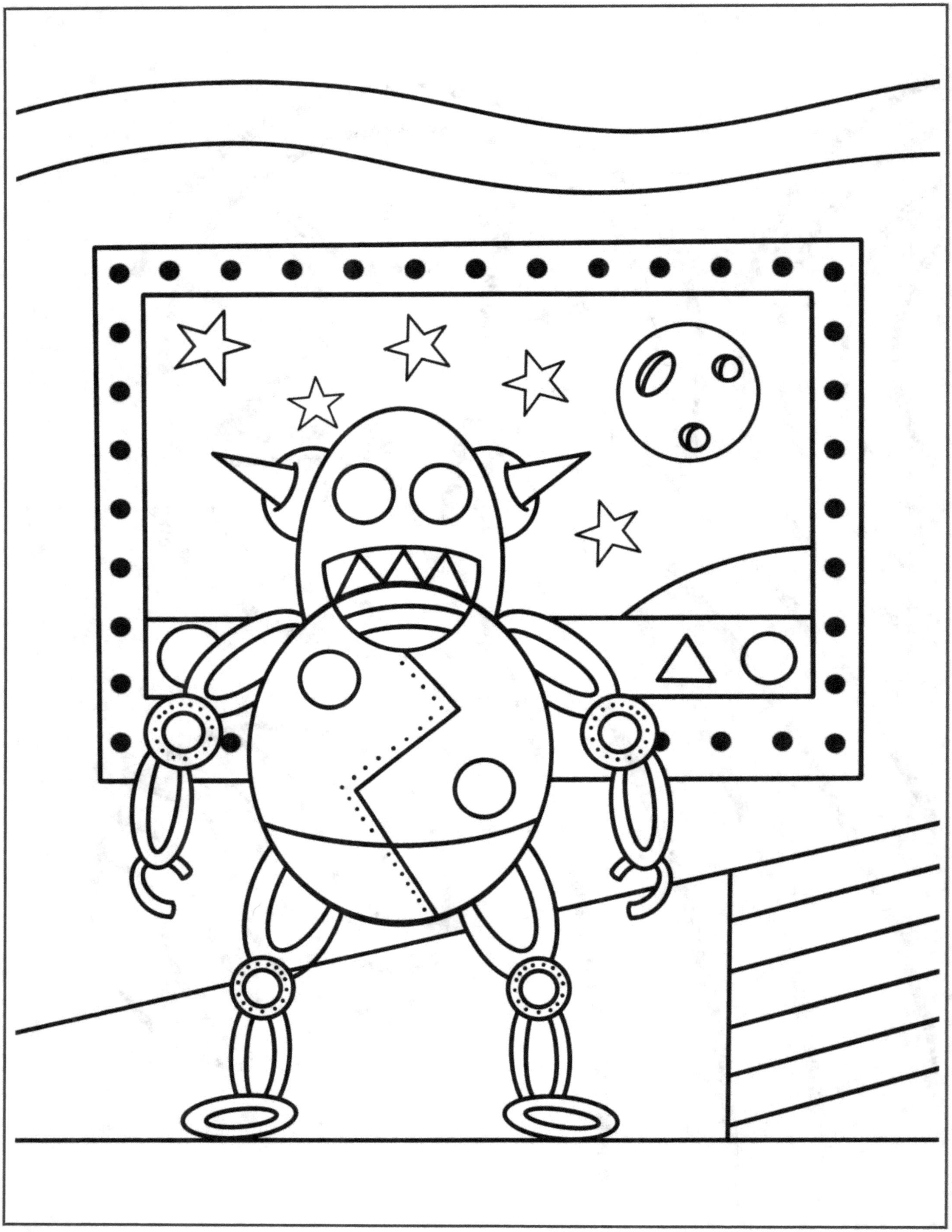

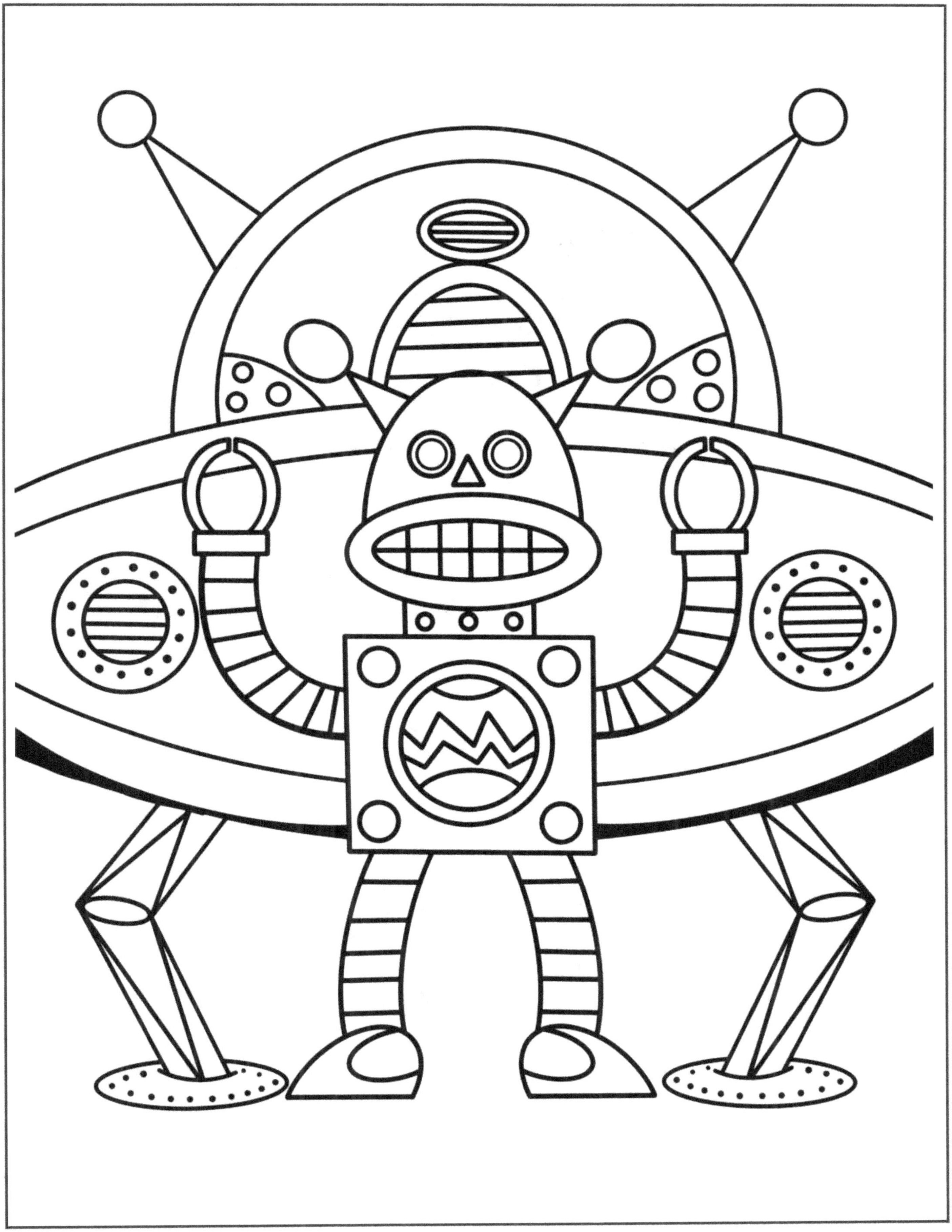

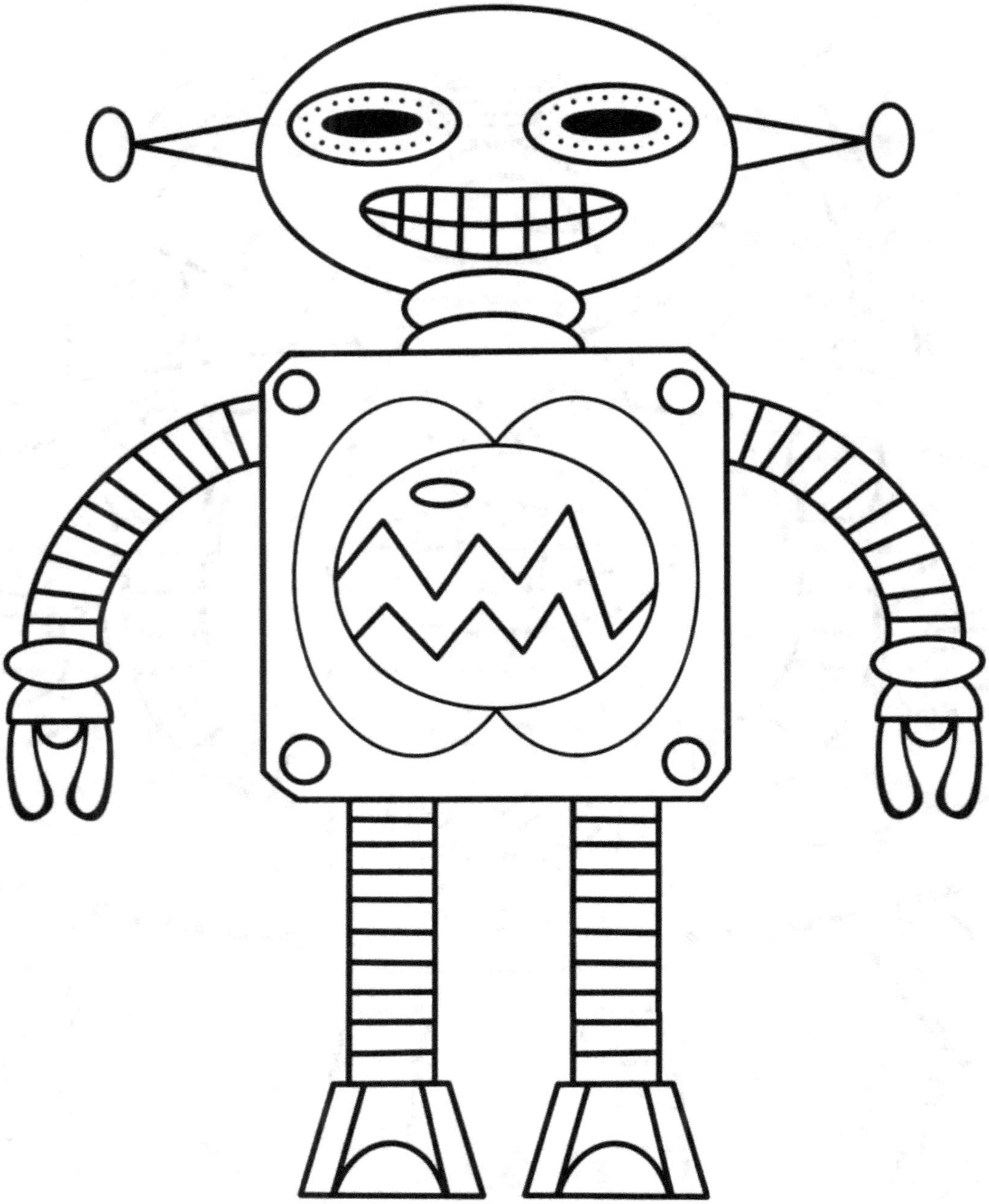

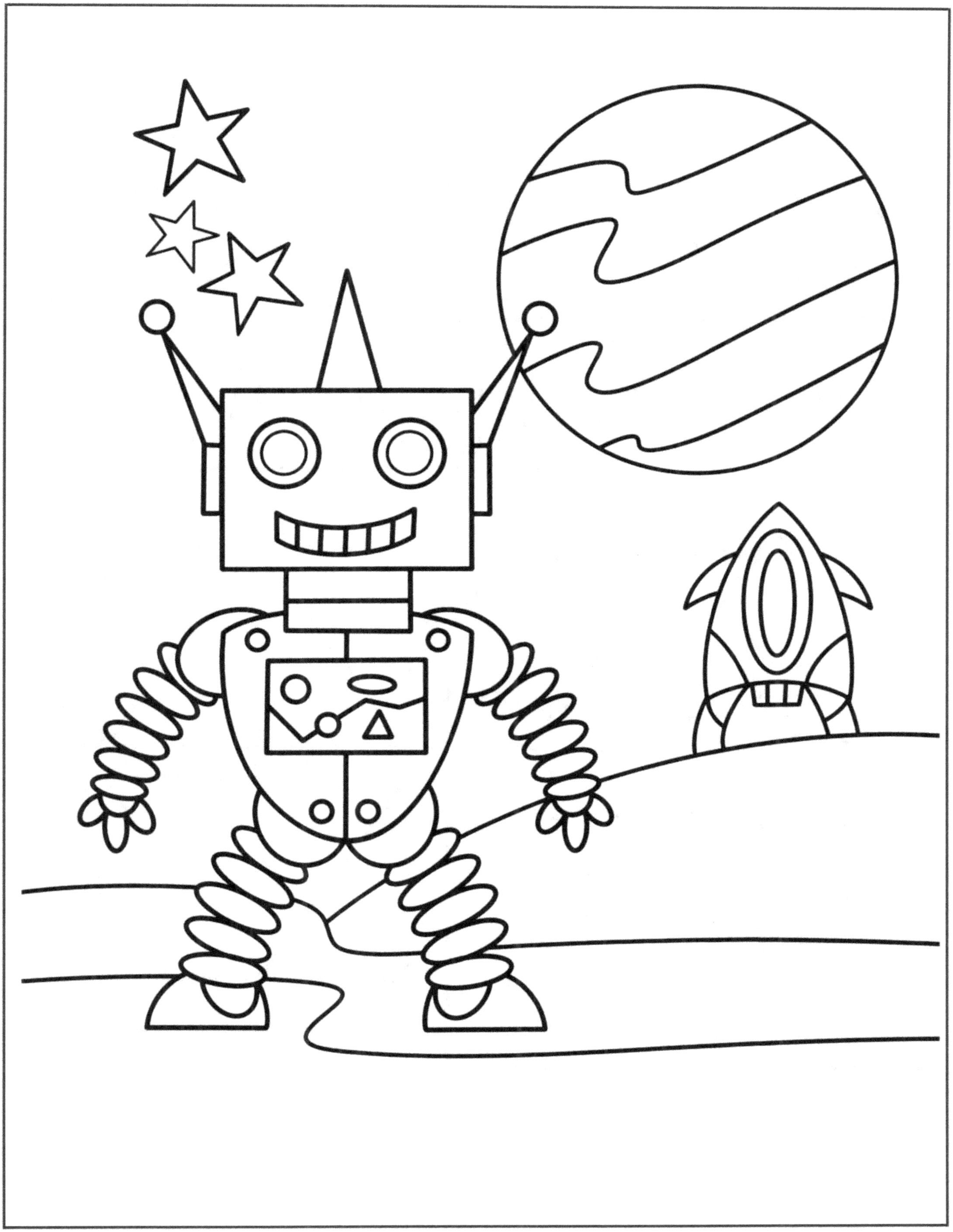

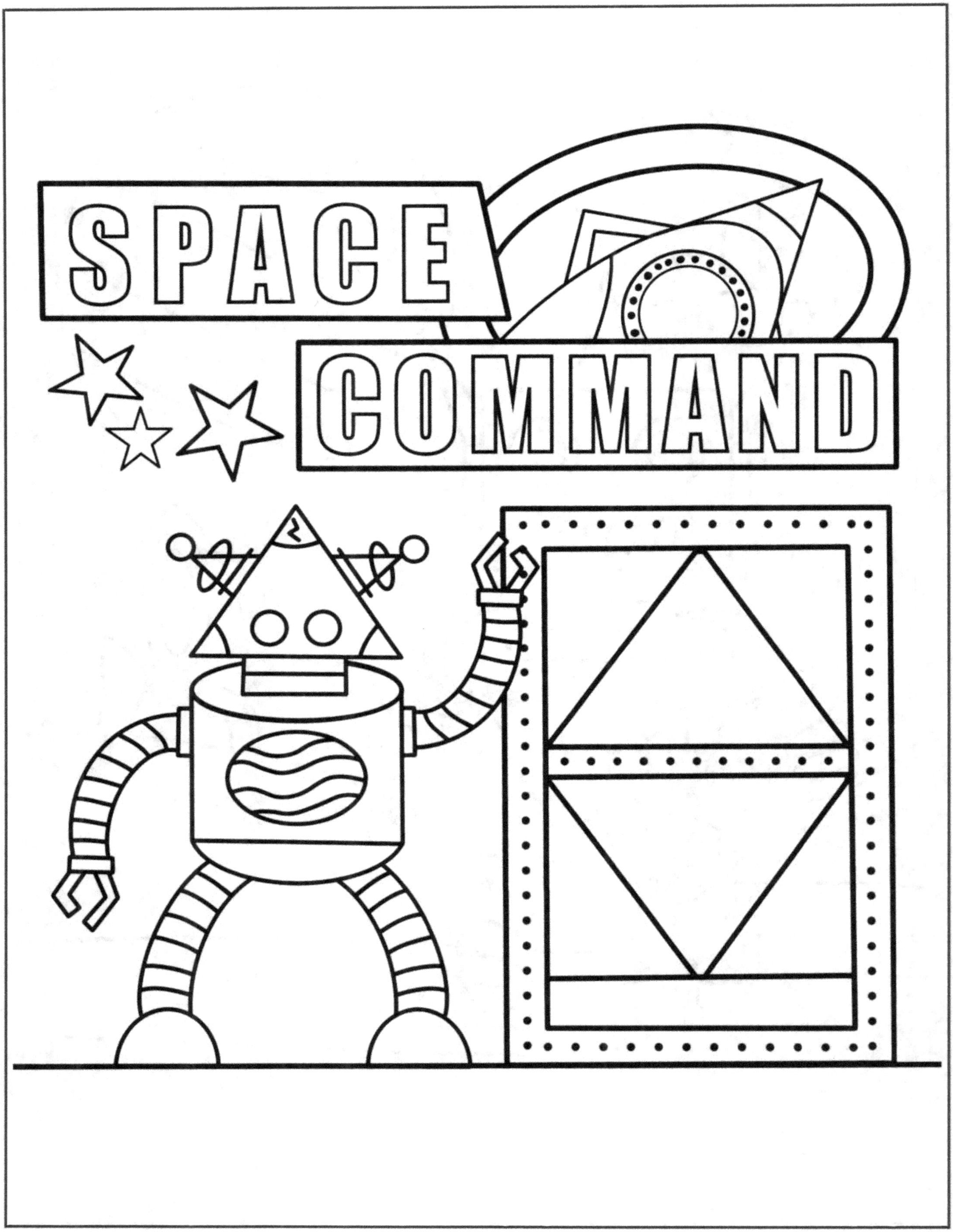
SPACE
COMMAND

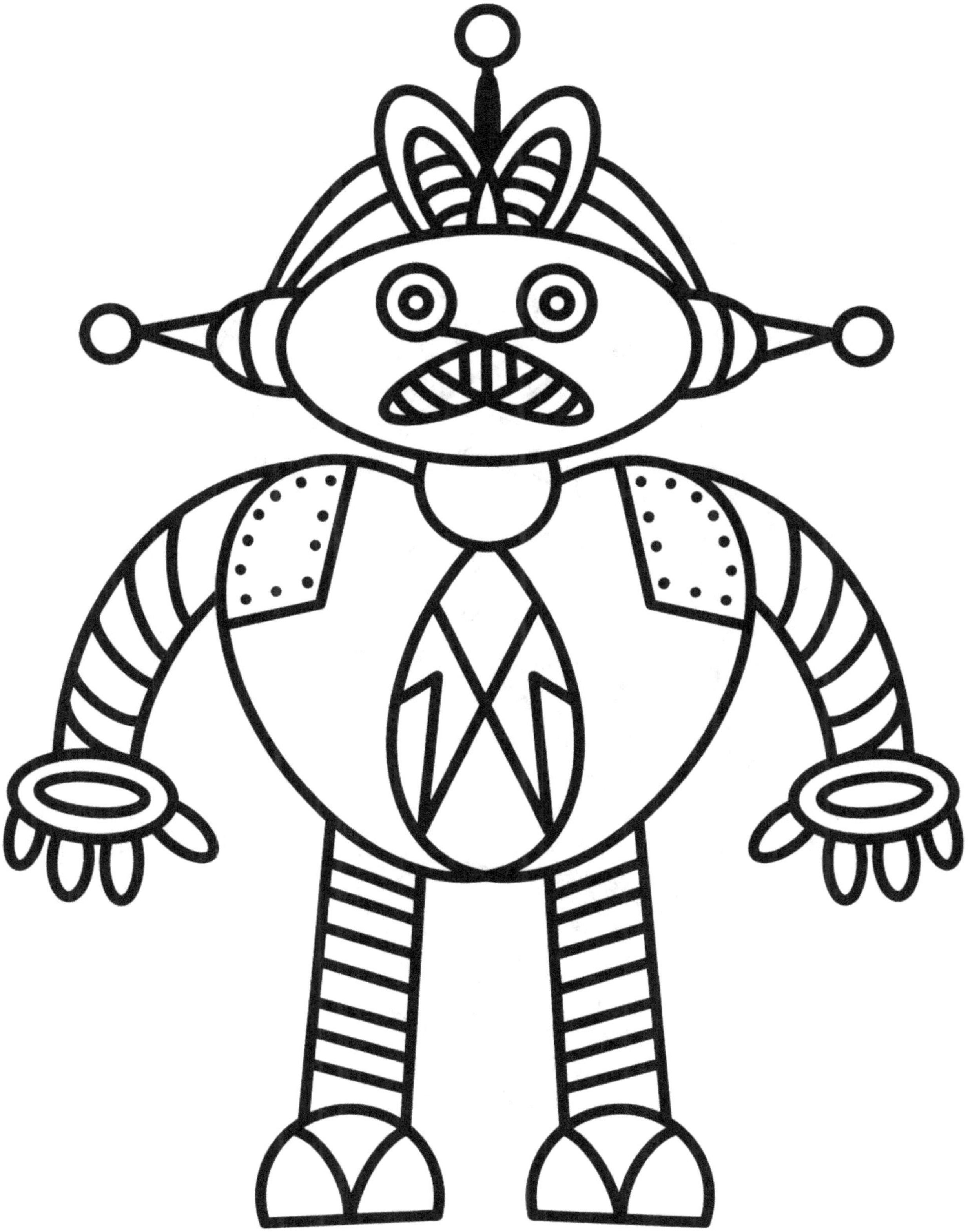

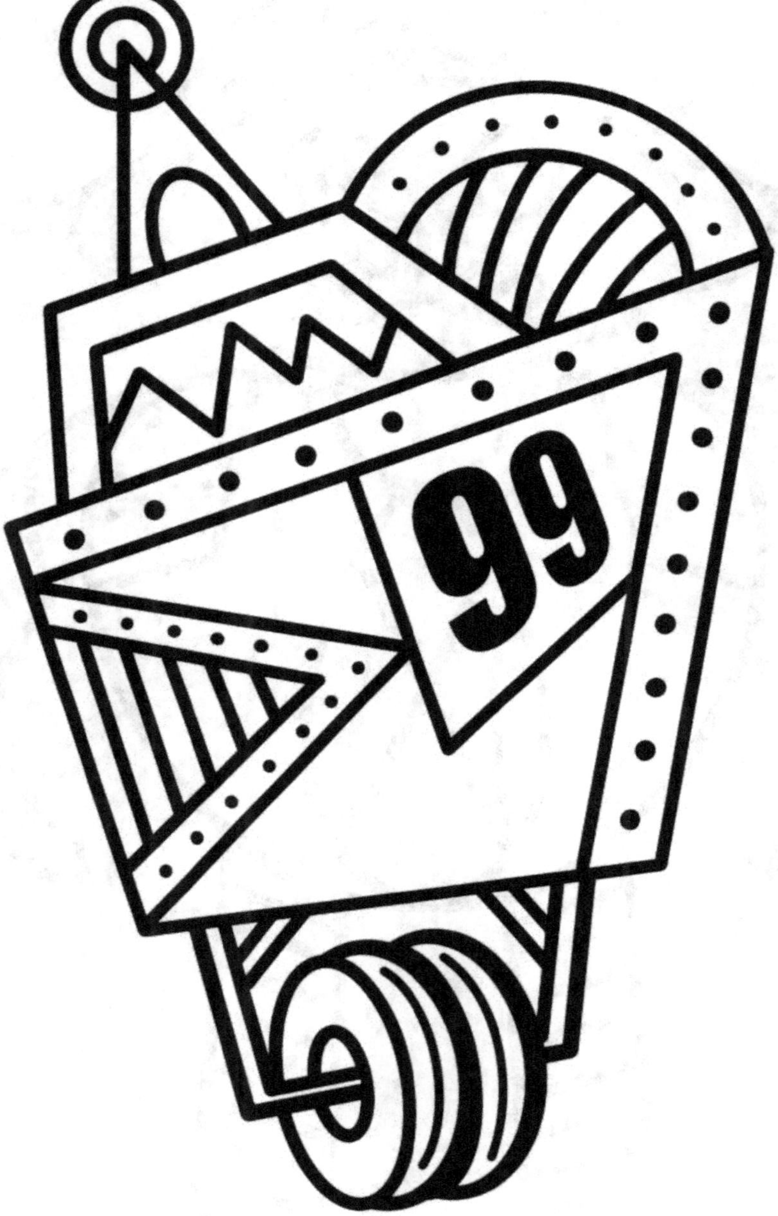
99

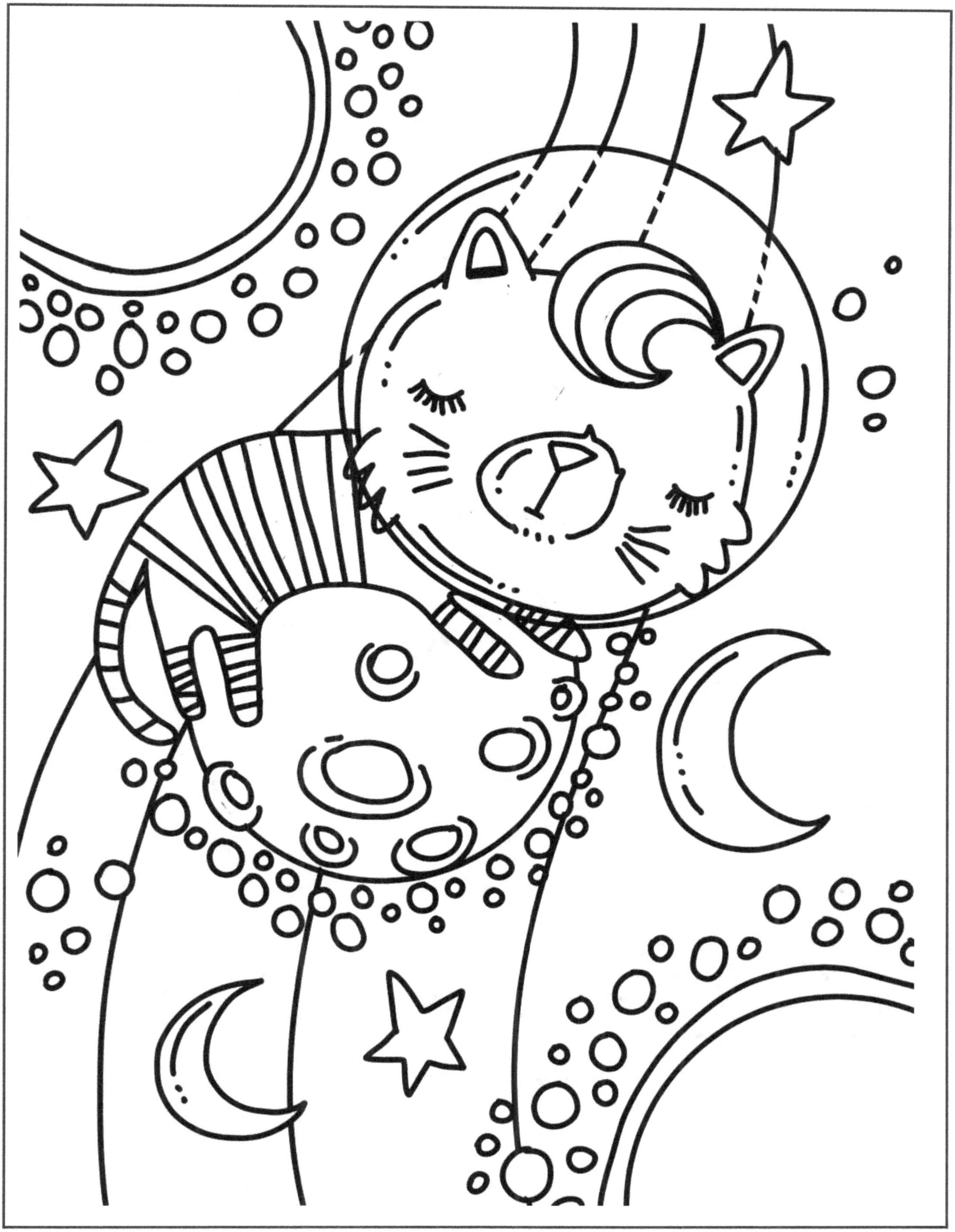

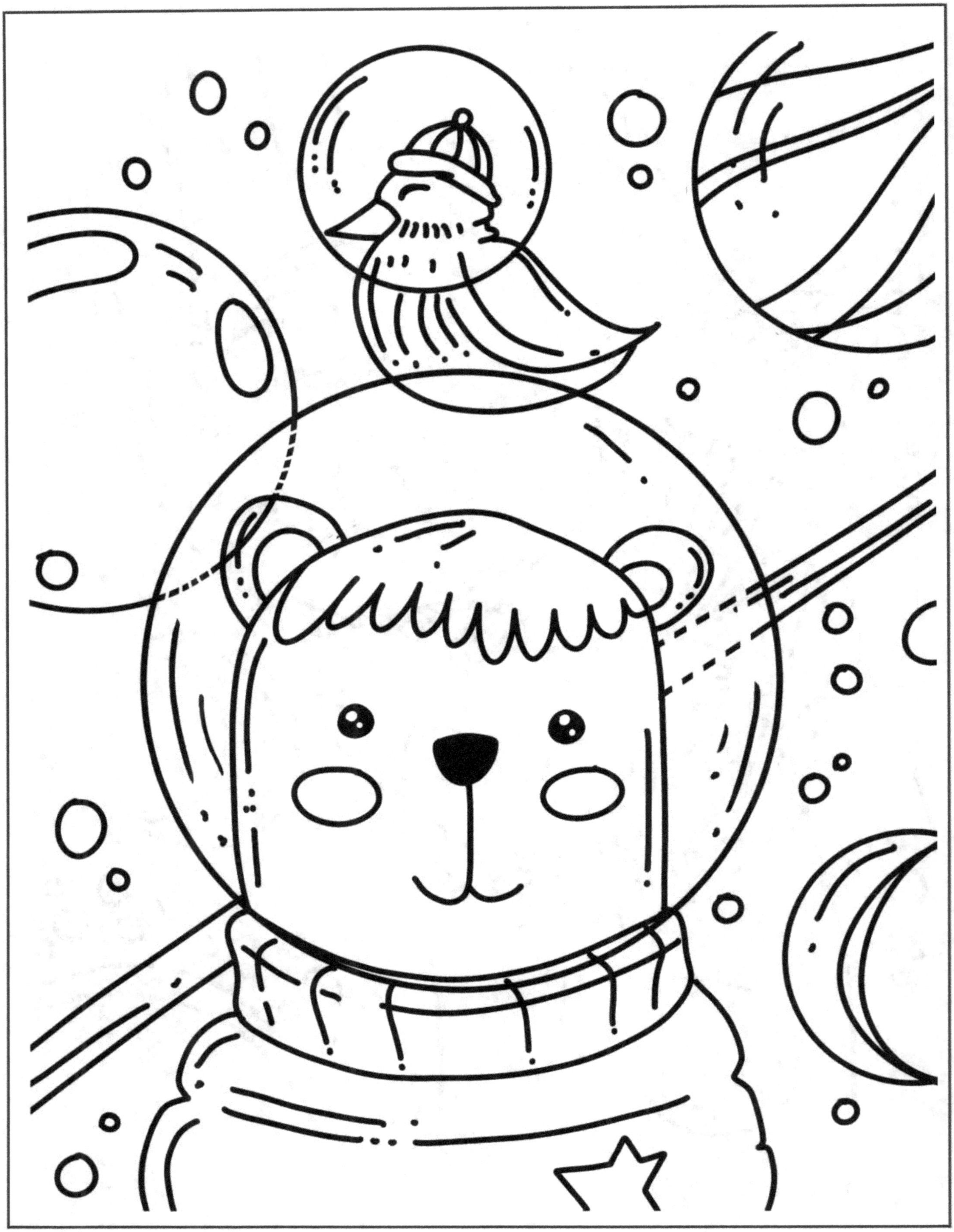

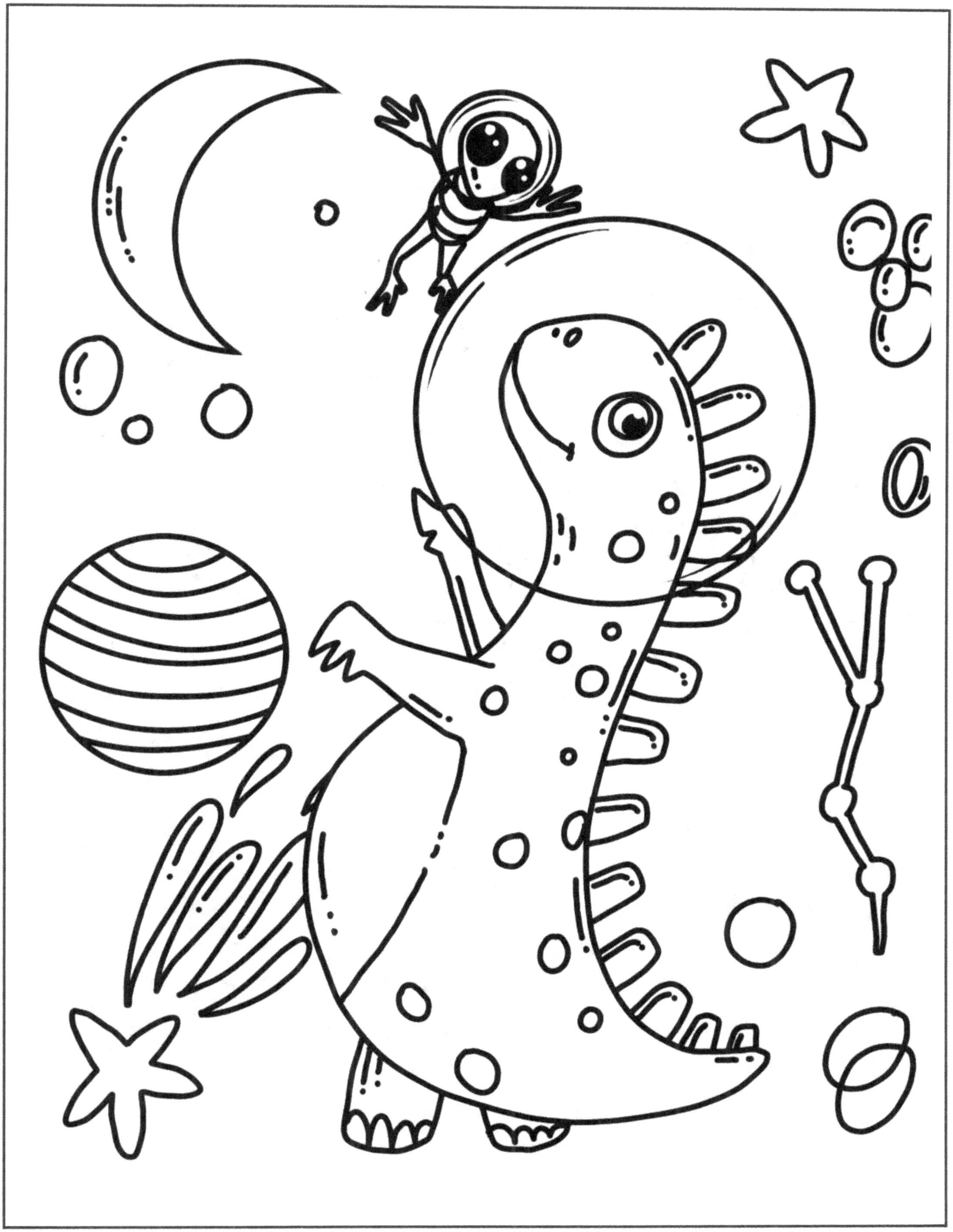

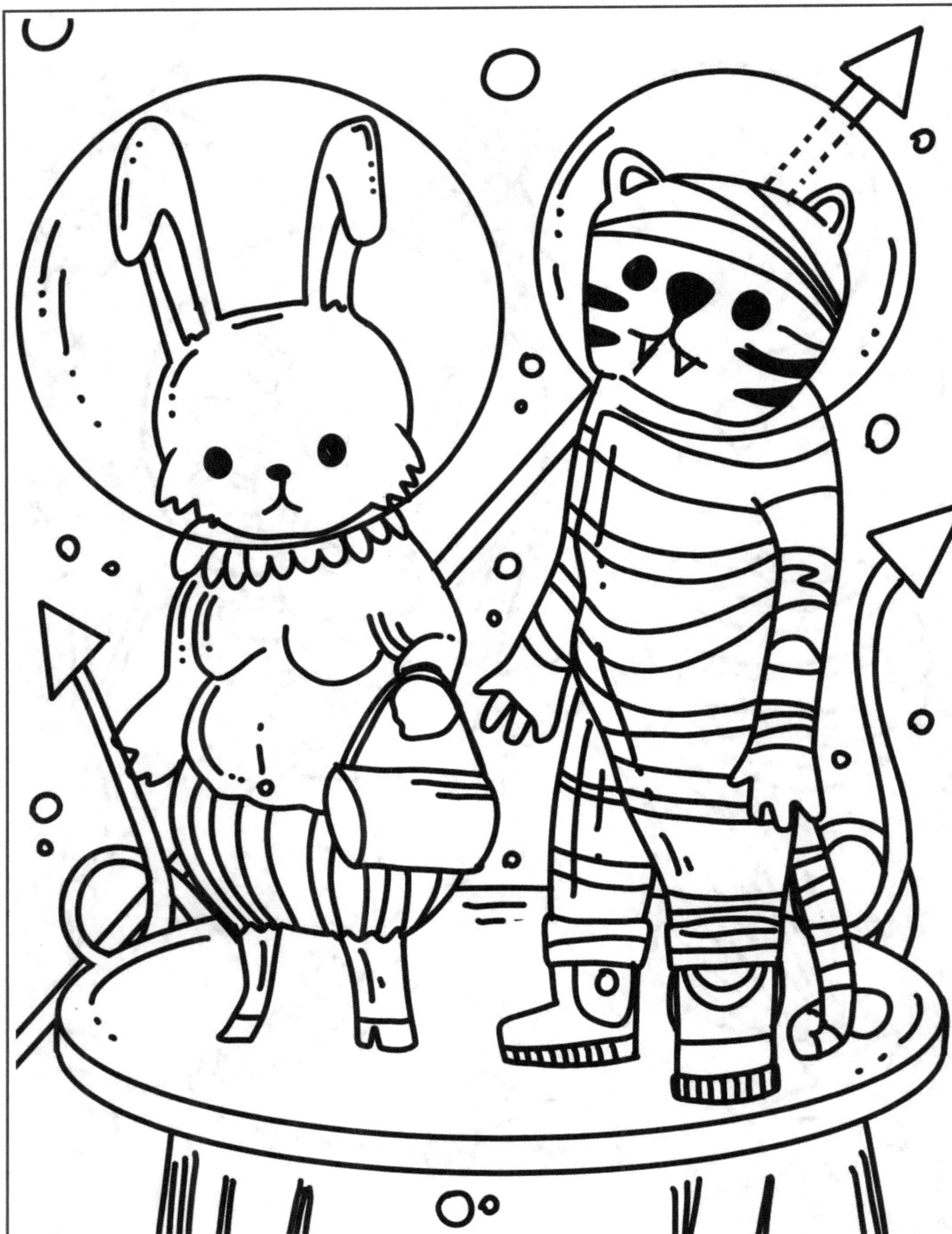

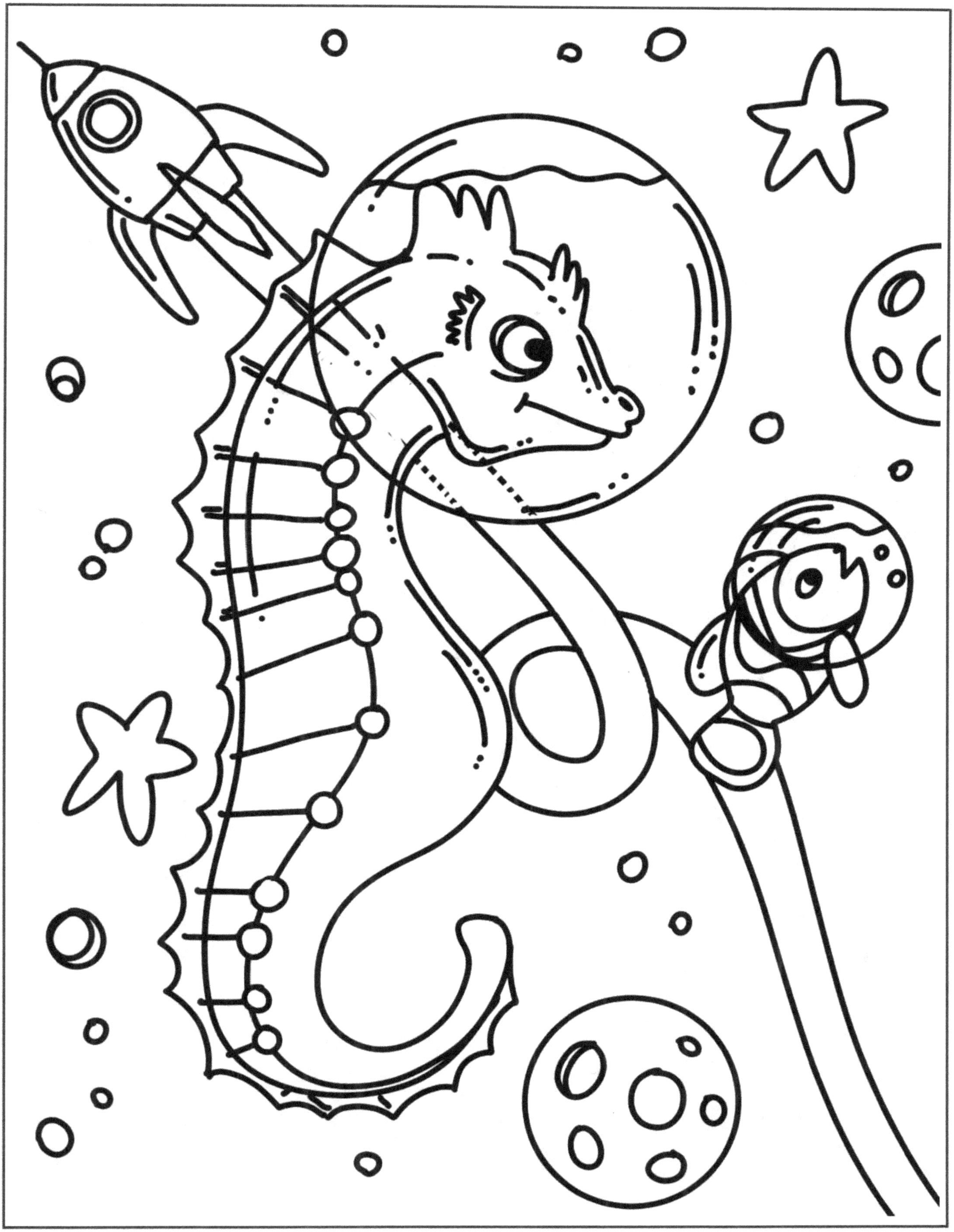

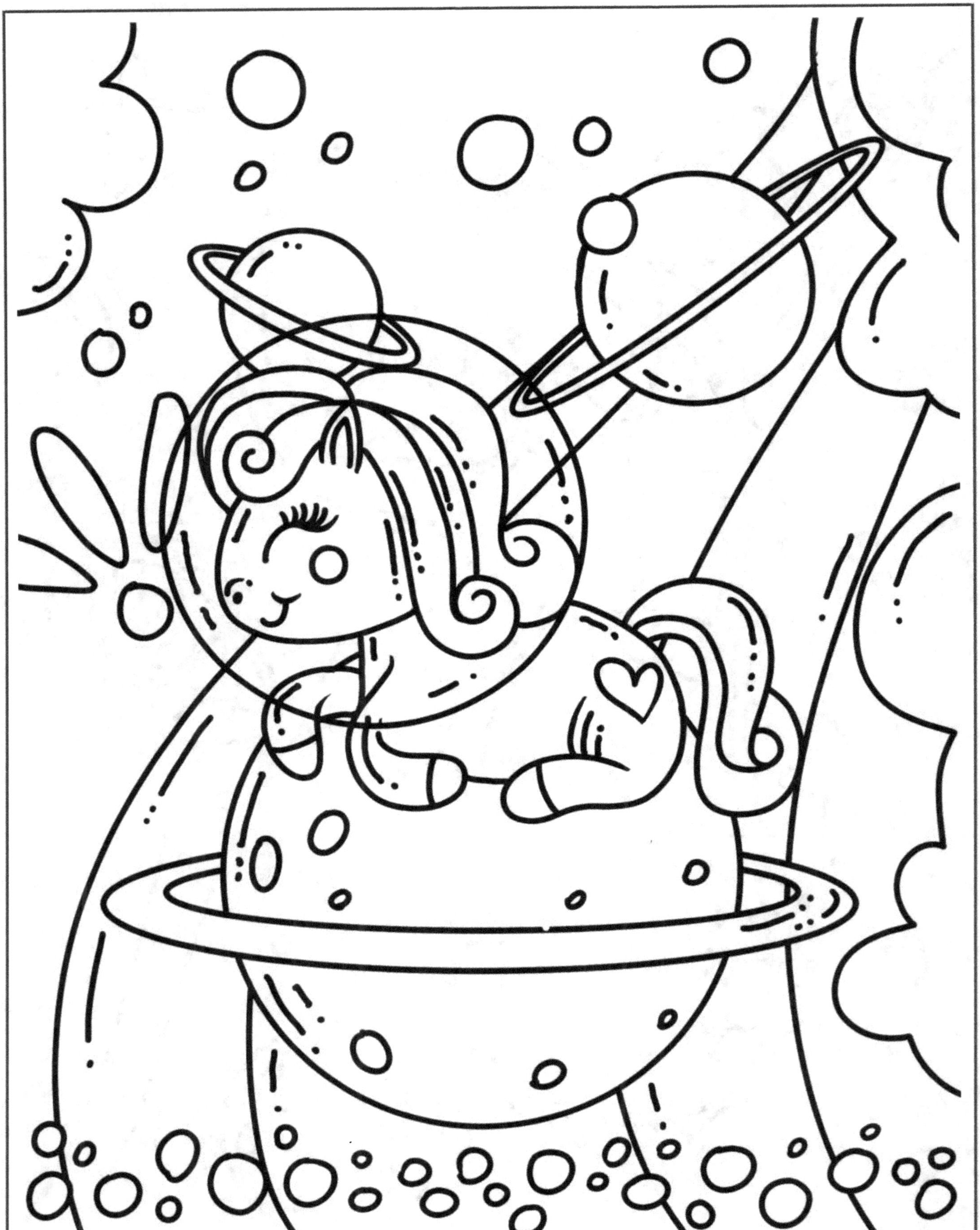

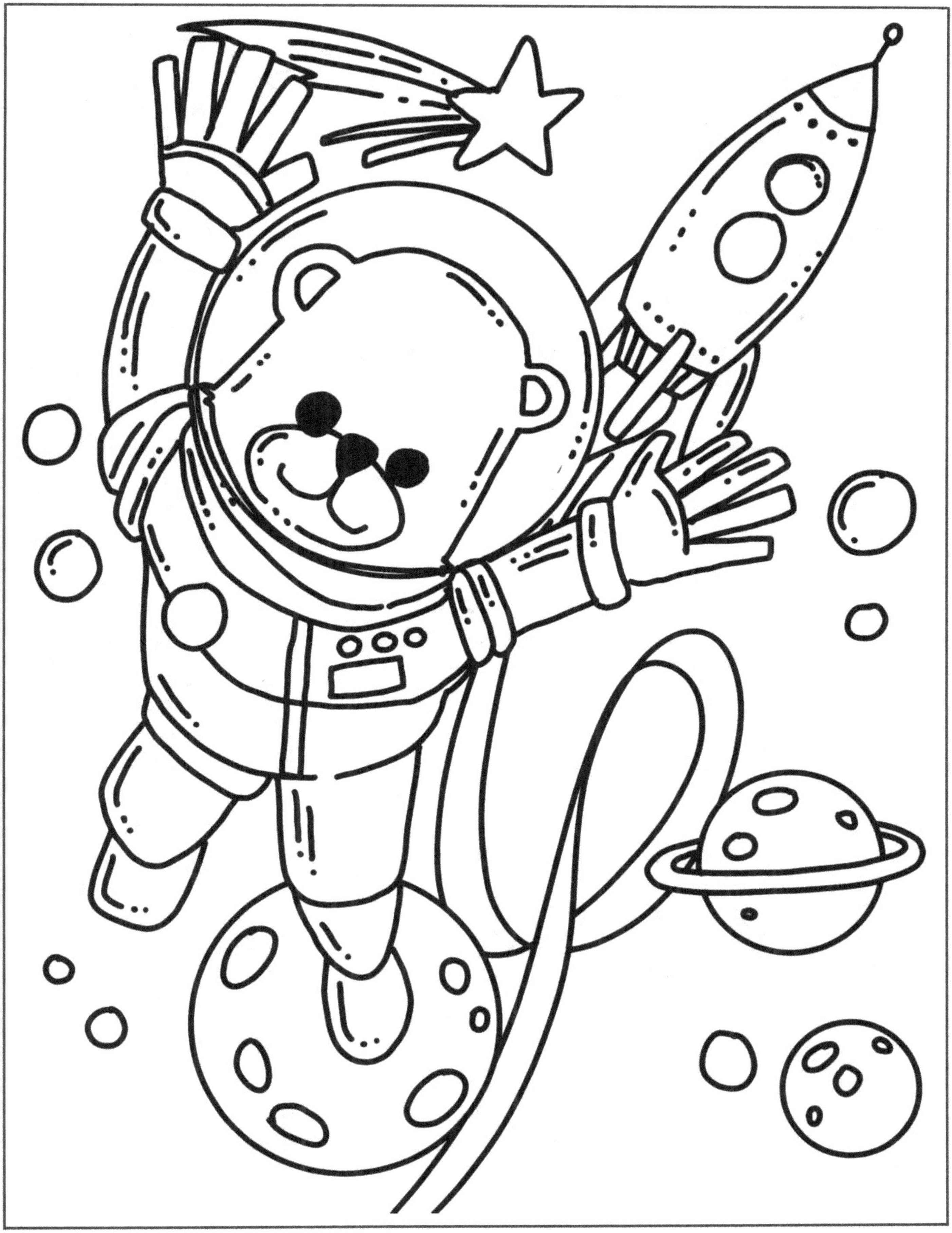

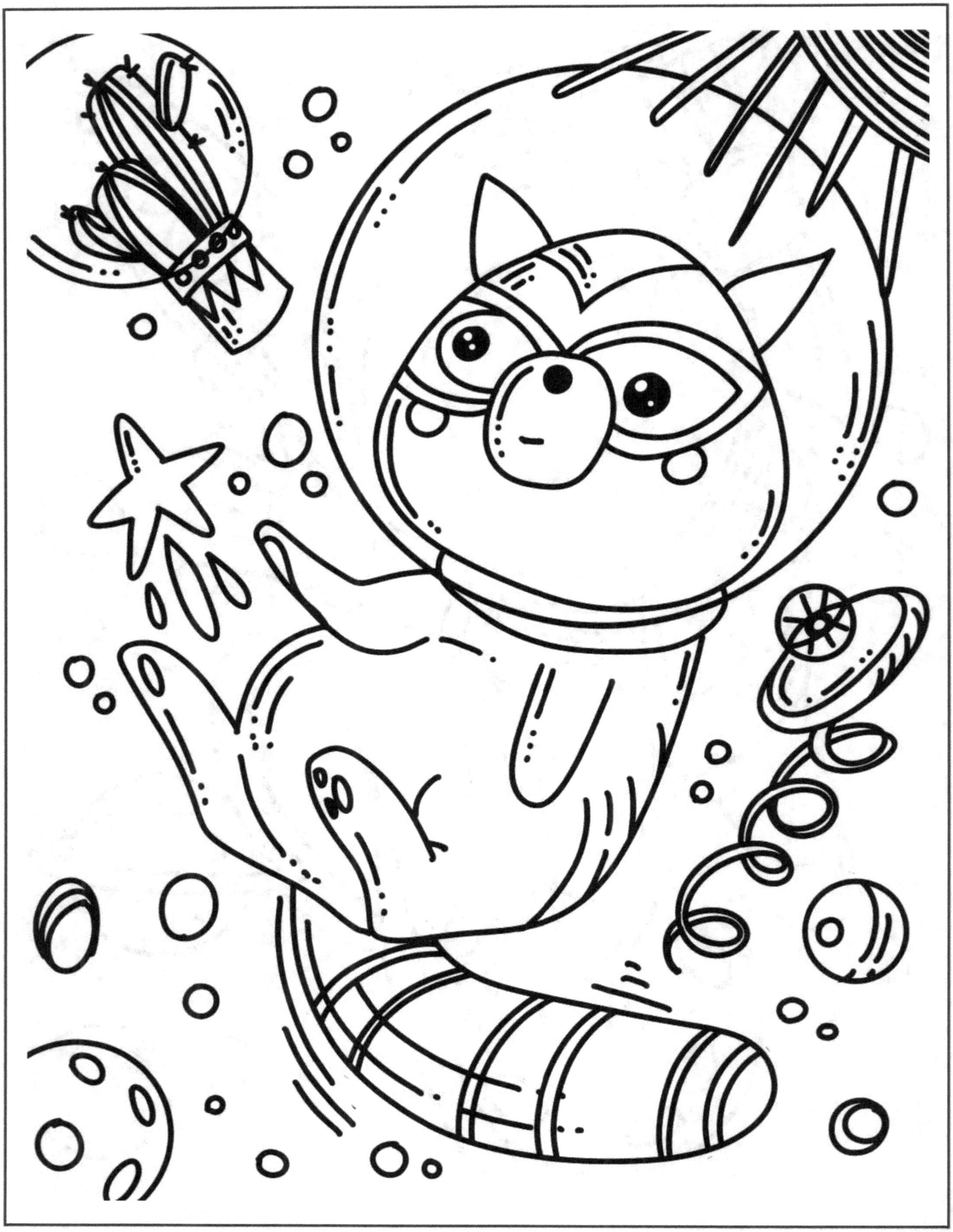

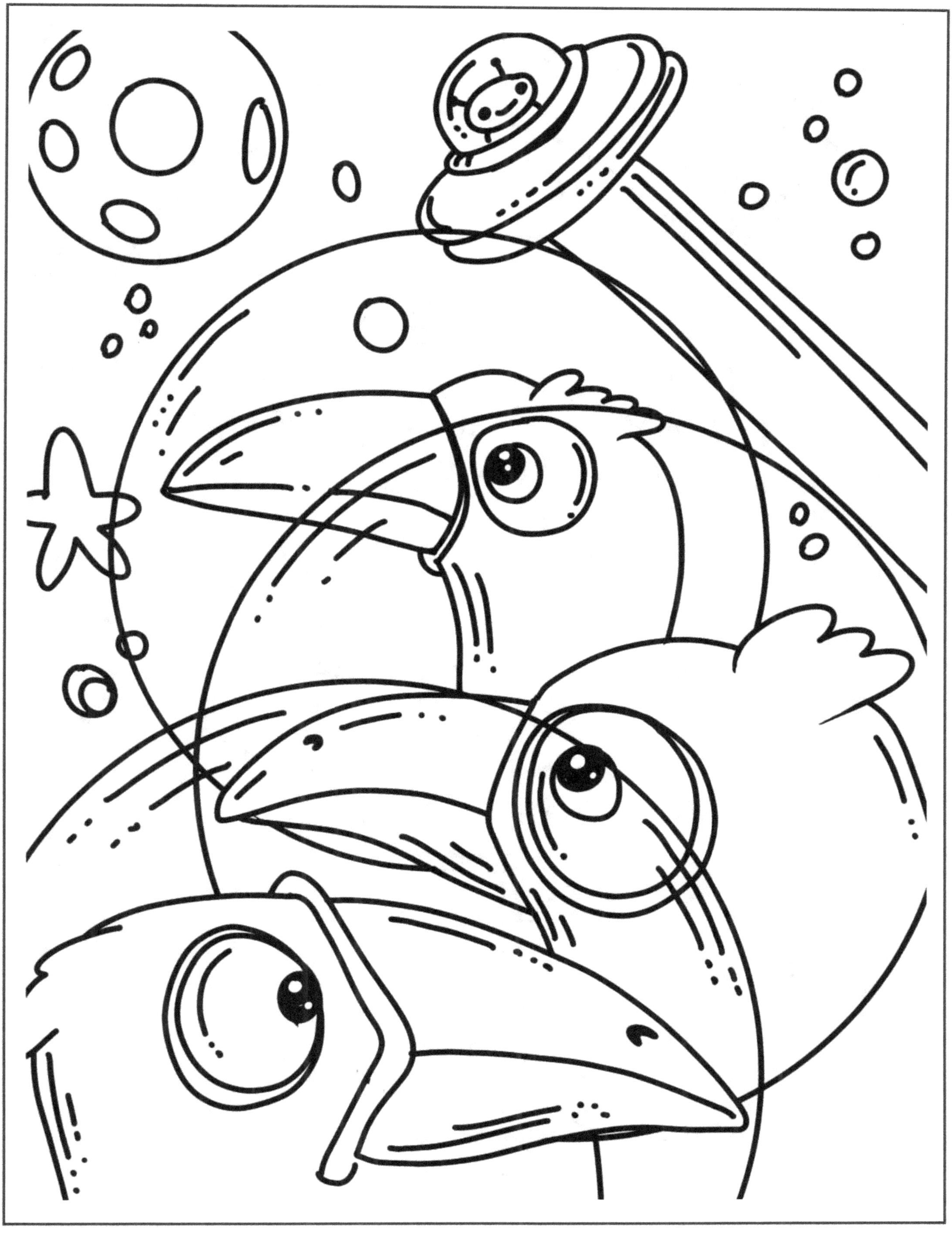

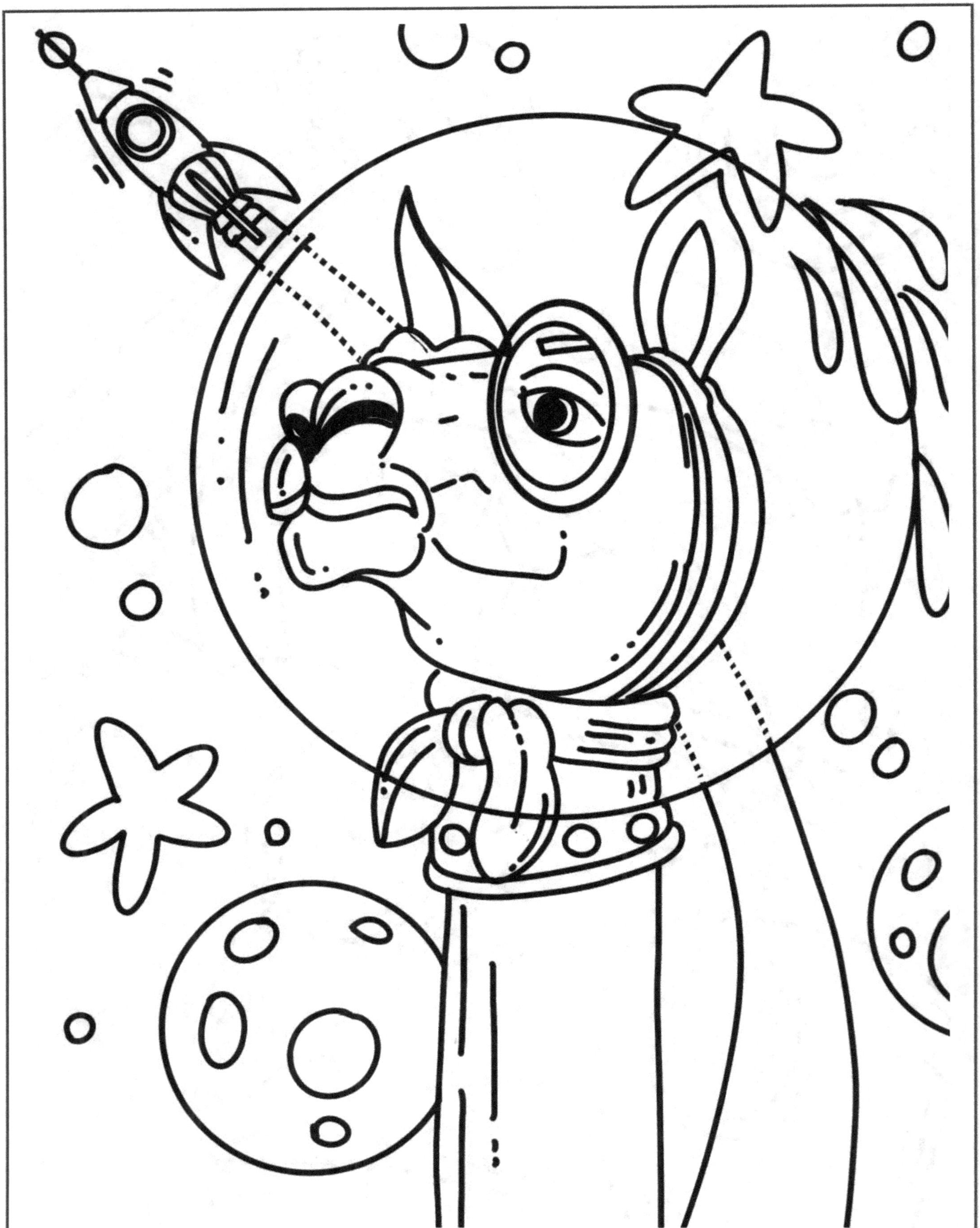

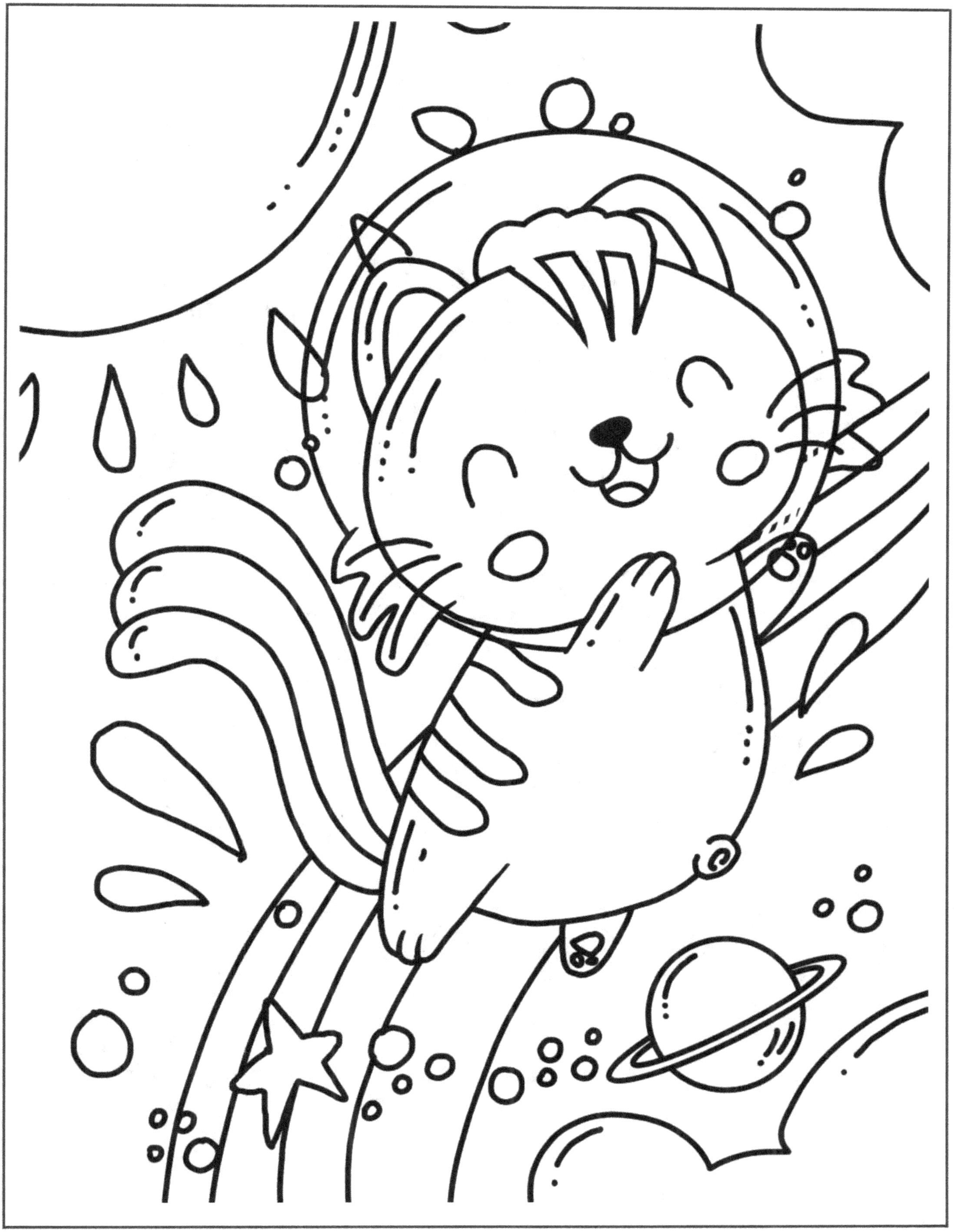

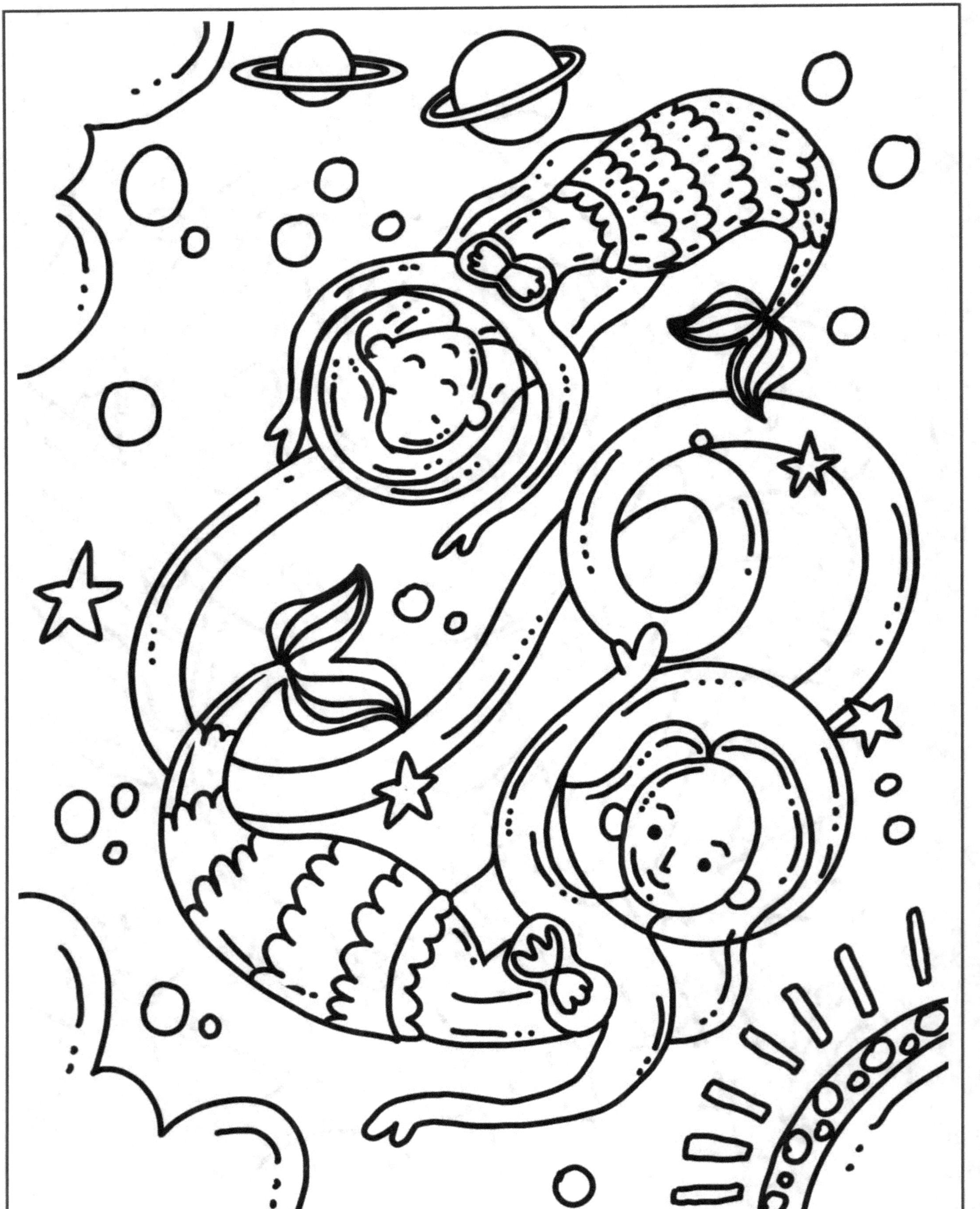

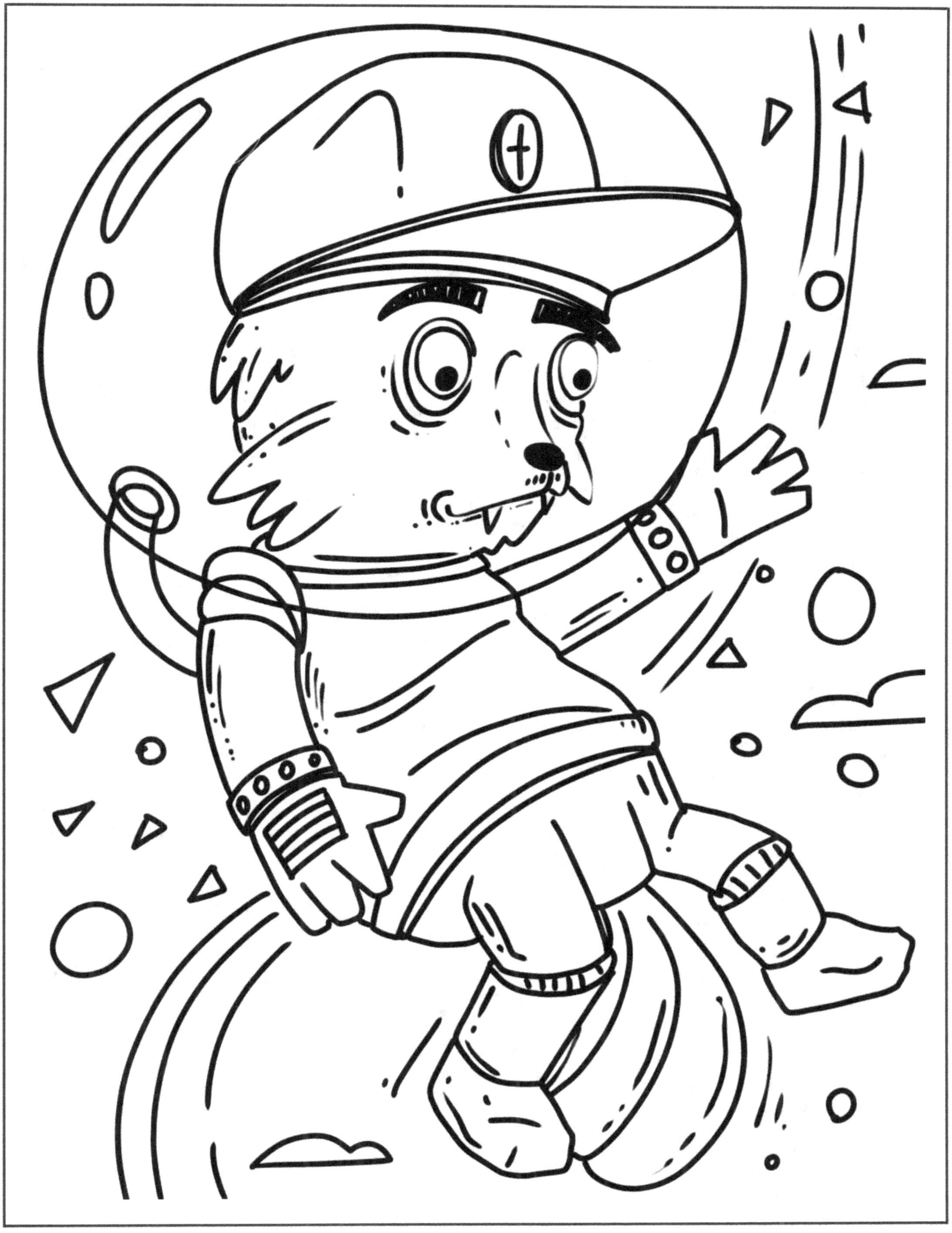

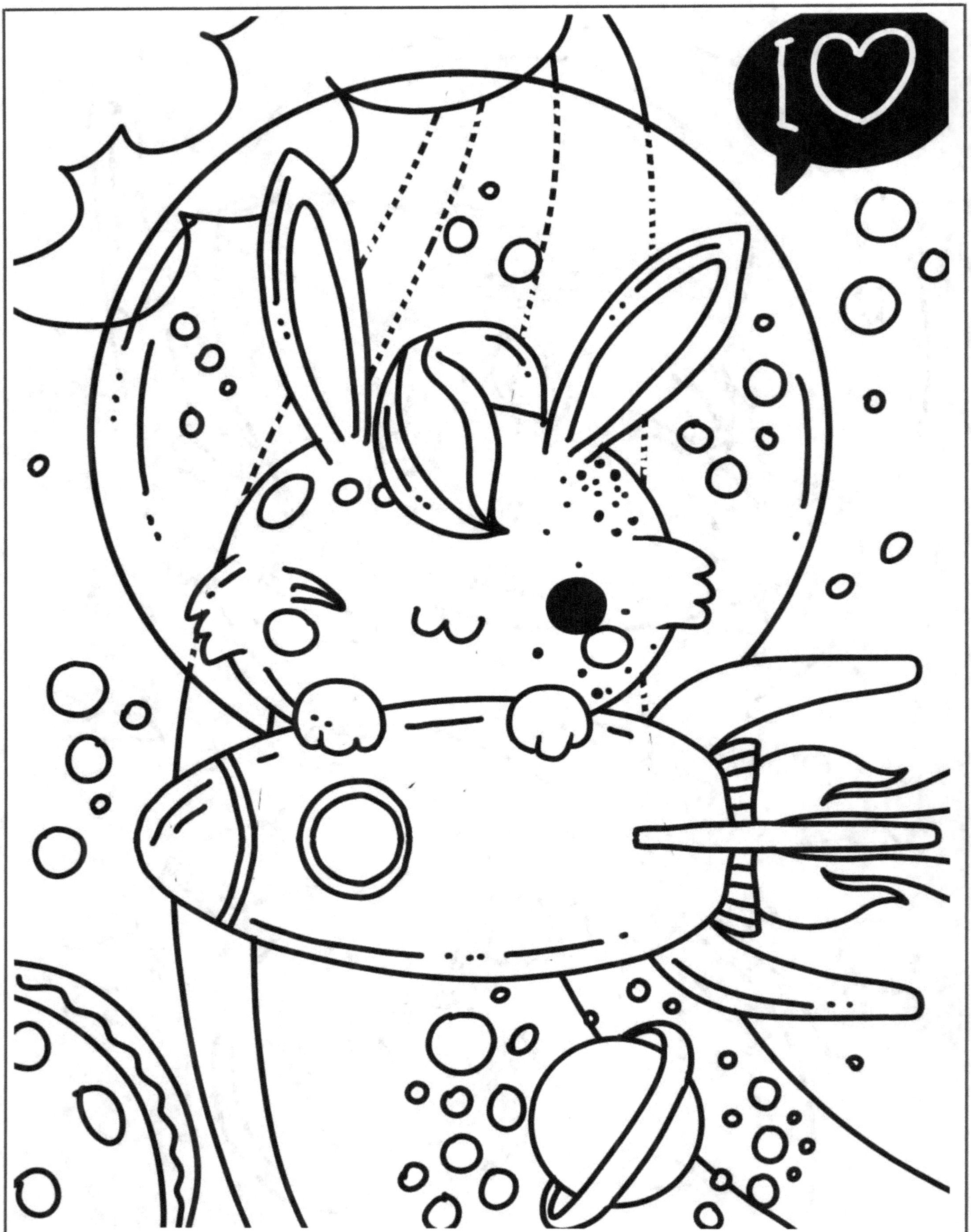
I ♡

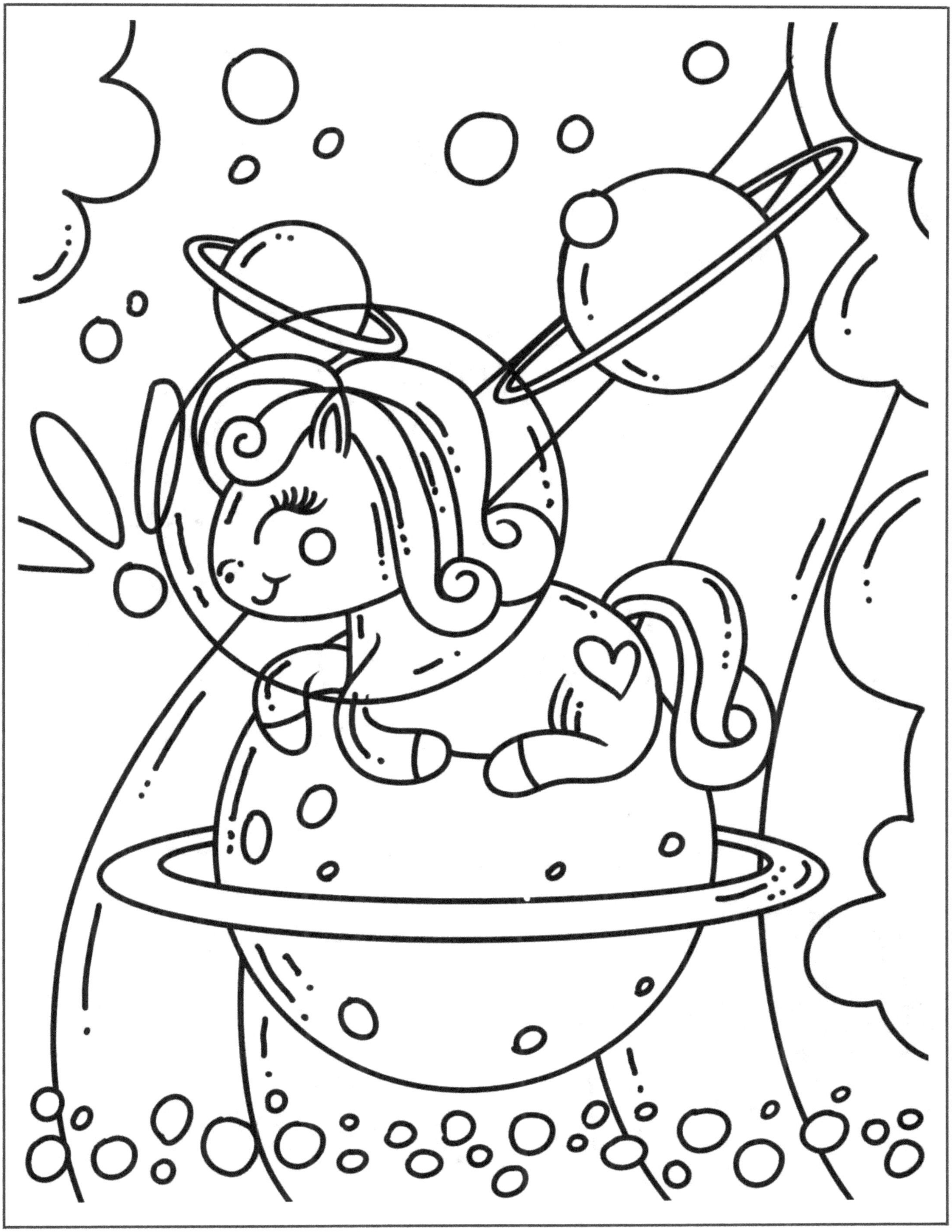

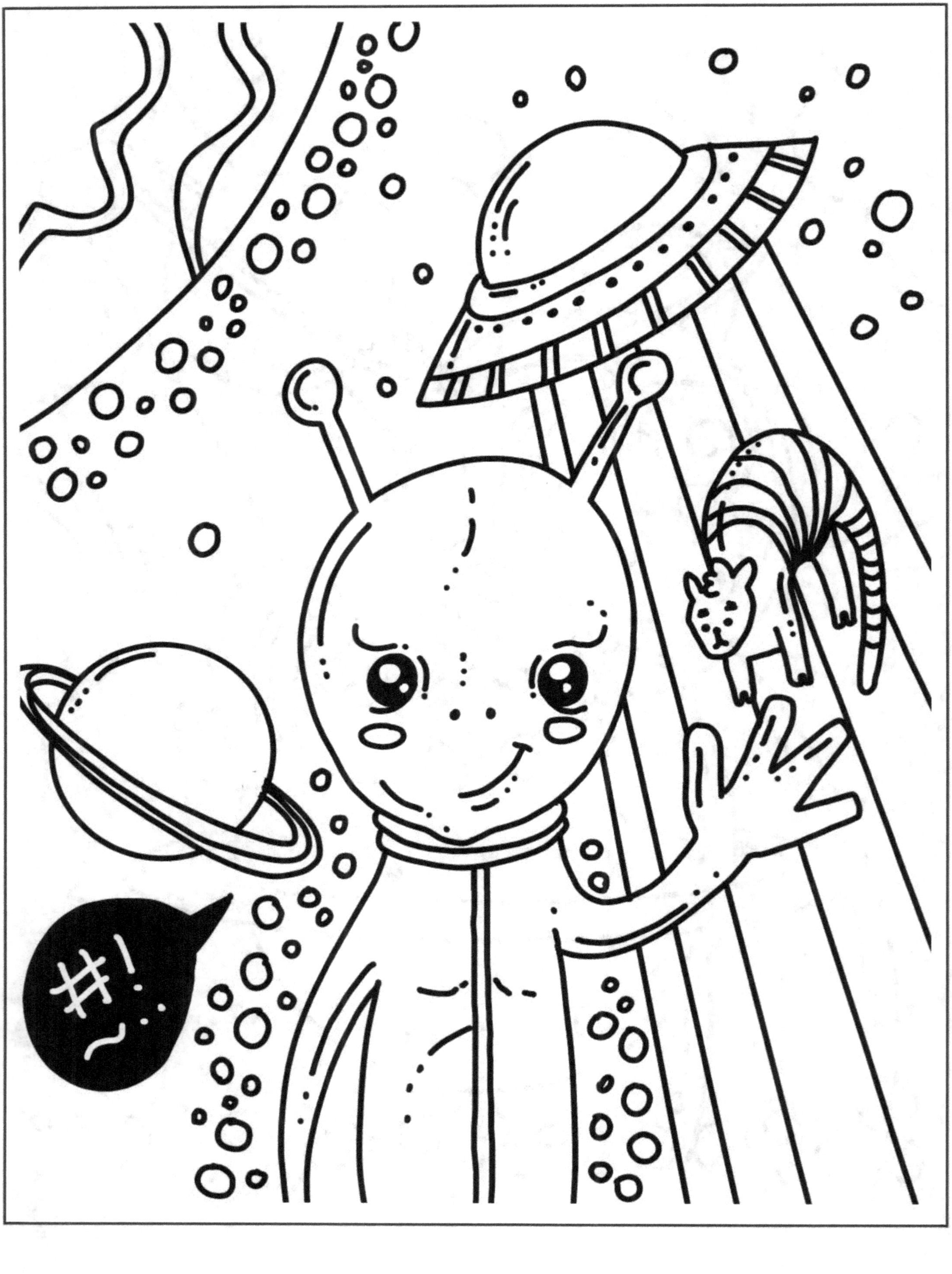

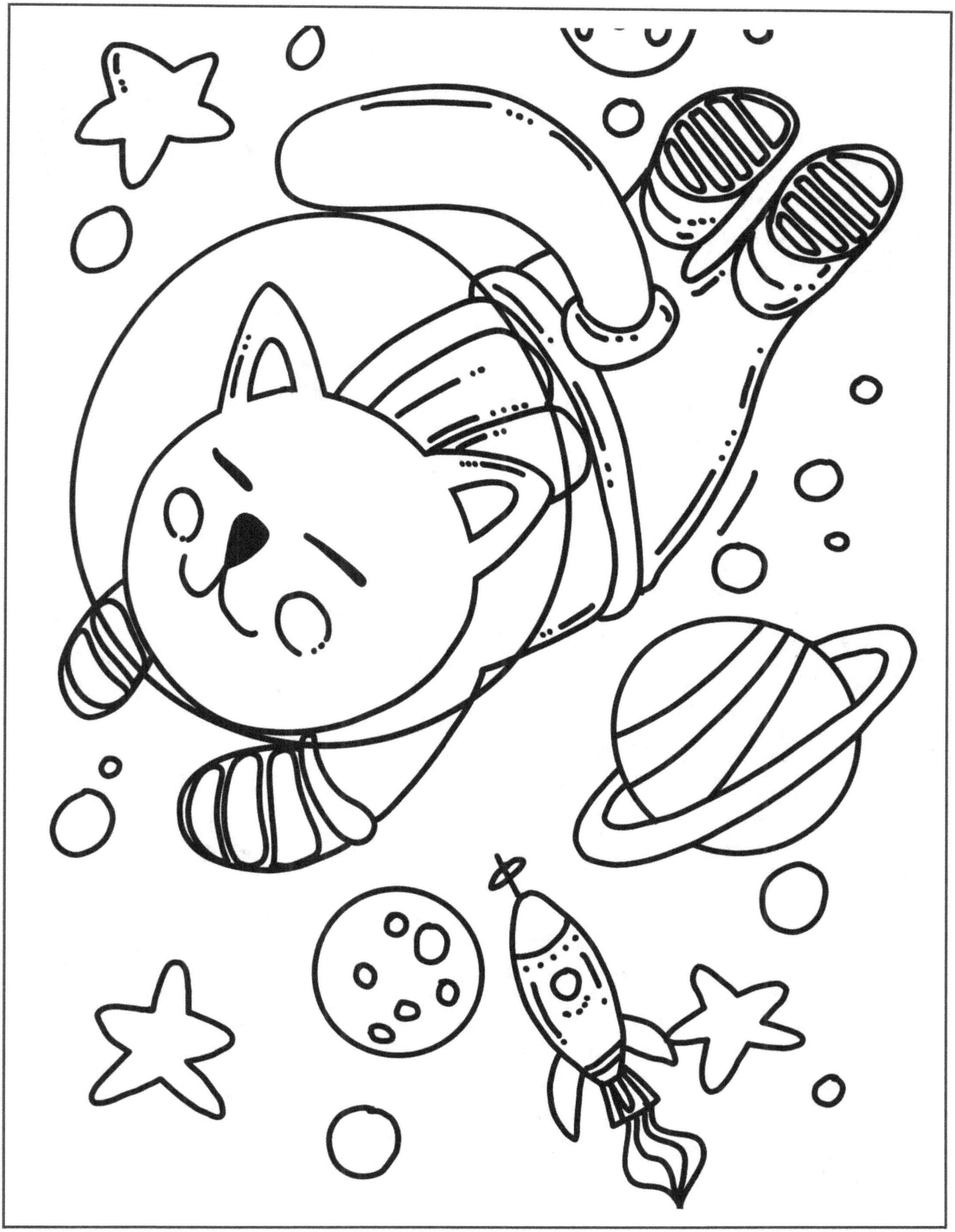

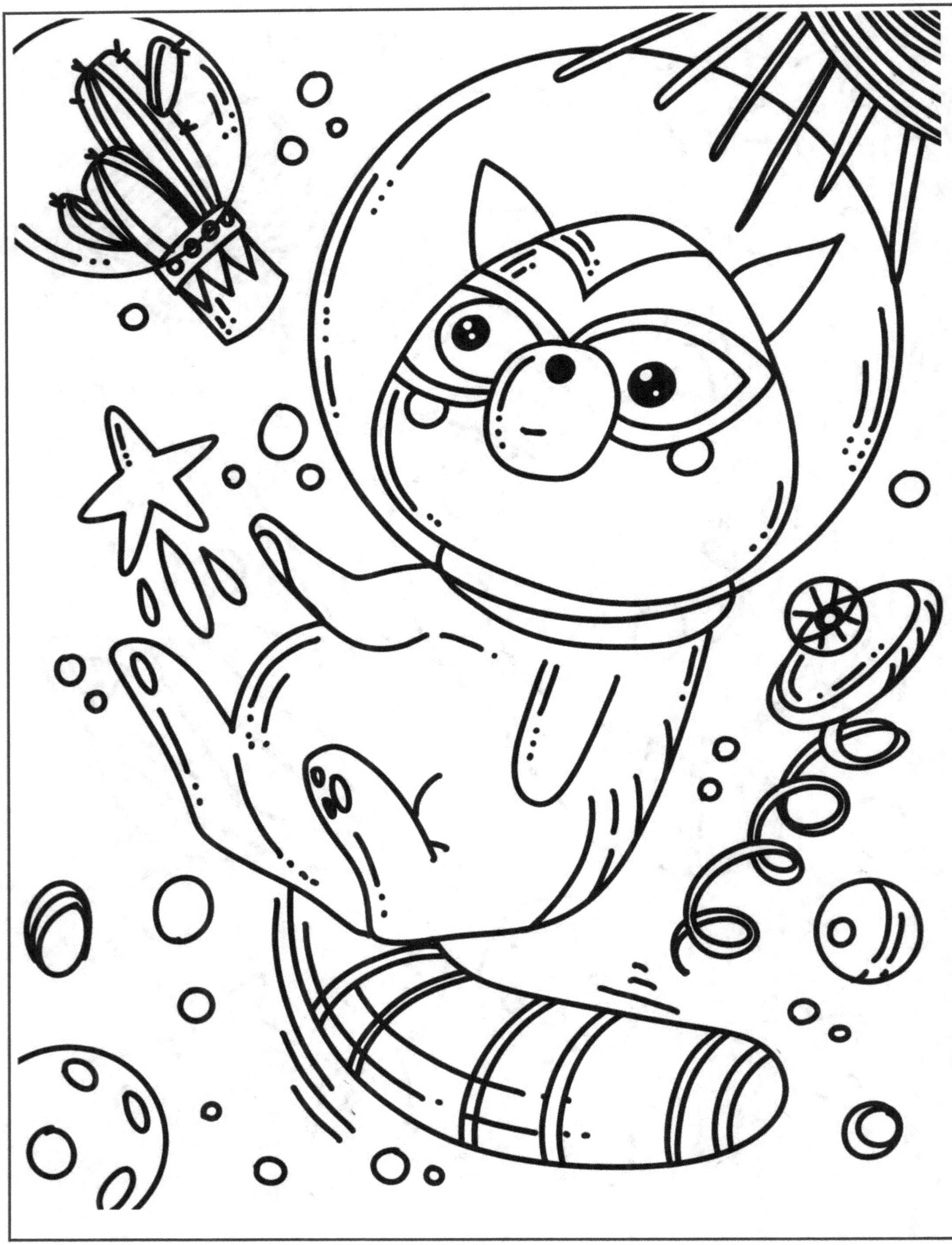

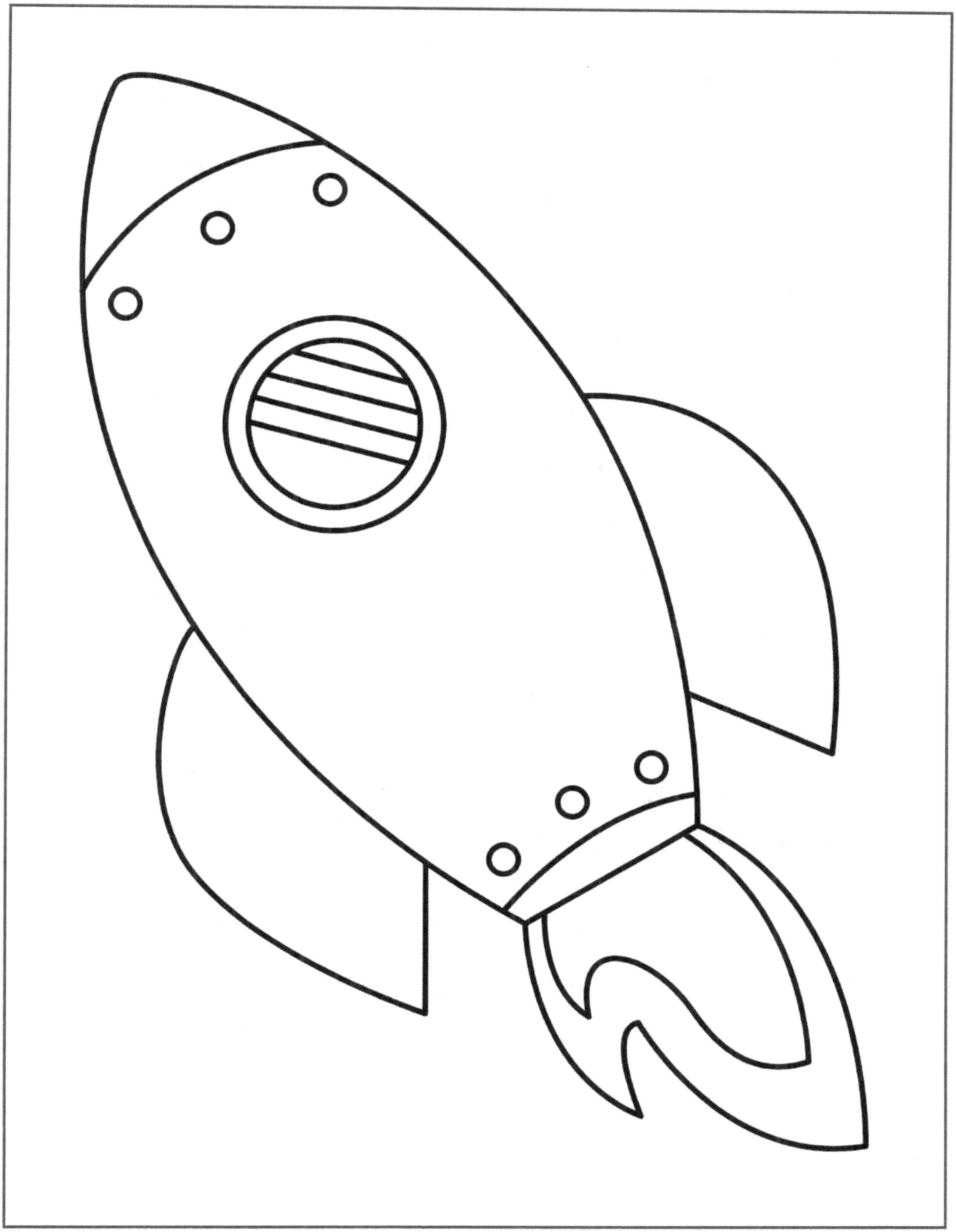

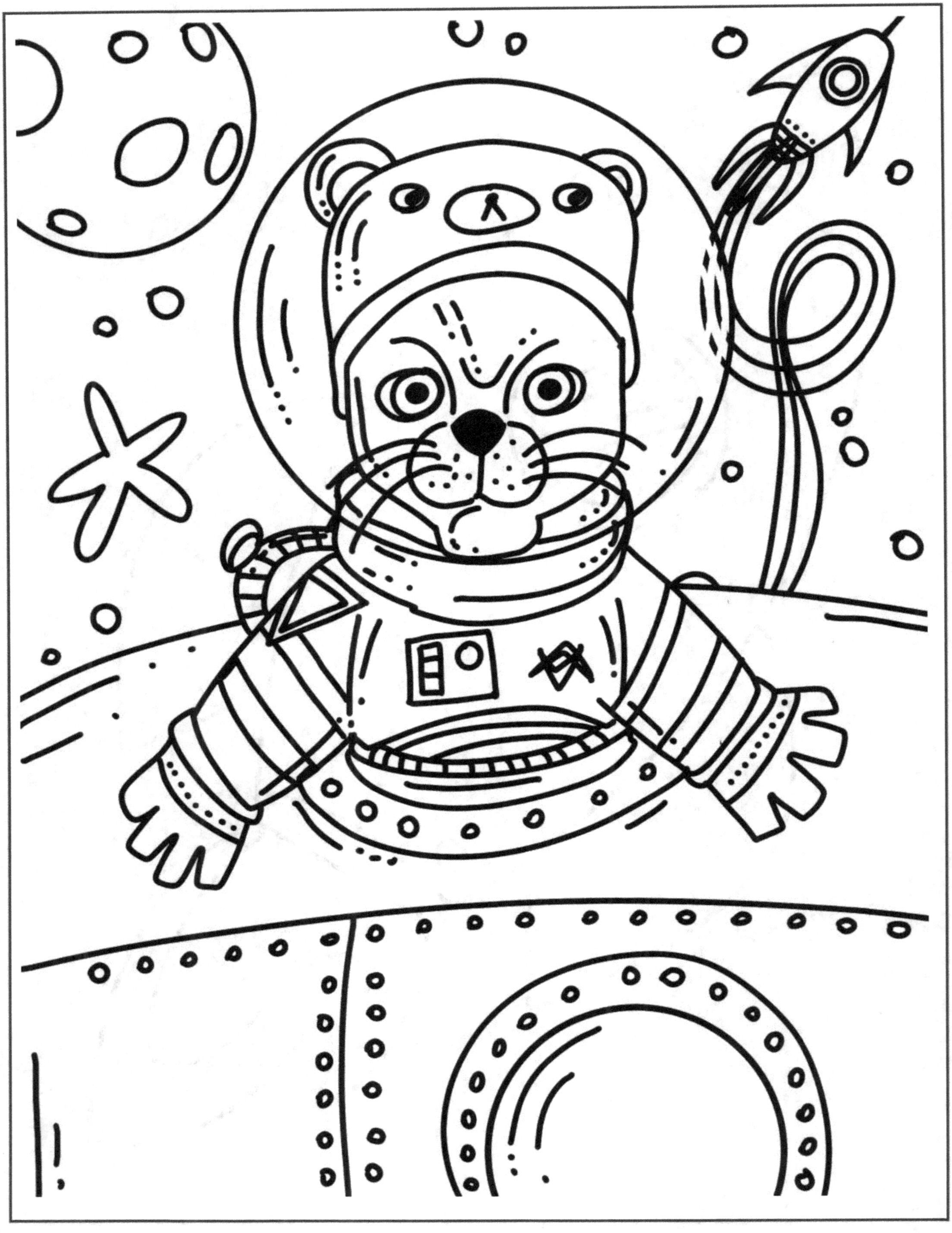

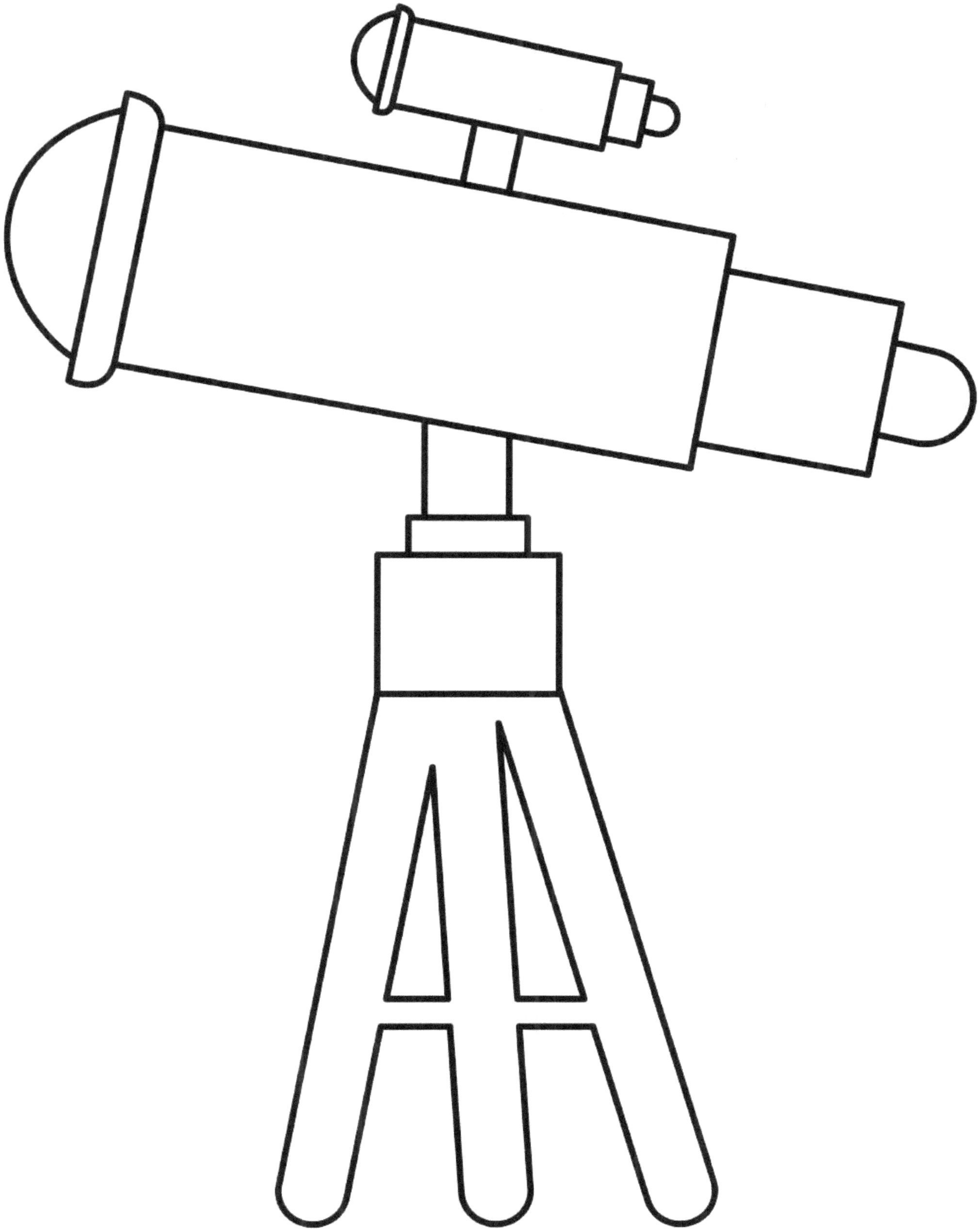

www.ingramcontent.com/pod-product-compliance
Lightning Source LLC
Chambersburg PA
CBHW080905220526
45466CB00011BA/3471
* 9 7 9 8 5 9 1 0 9 3 6 3 1 *